City BLOCKS

LEISURE ARTS, INC.
Little Rock, Arkansas

EDITORIAL STAFF

Vice President and Editor-in-Chief:
   Susan White Sullivan
Quilt and Craft Publications Director:
   Cheryl Johnson
Special Projects Director: Susan Frantz Wiles
Director of E-Commerce: Mark Hawkins
Art Publications Director: Rhonda Shelby
Technical Editor: Lisa Lancaster
Associate Editor: Frances Huddleston
Editorial Writer: Susan McManus Johnson
Art Category Manager: Lora Puls
Graphic Artists: Amy Temple, Jacob Casleton
   and Stacy Owens
Imaging Technician: Stephanie Johnson
Prepress Technician: Janie Marie Wright
Photography Manager: Katherine Laughlin
Contributing Photographer: Ken West
Contributing Photo Stylist: Sondra Daniel
Publishing Systems Administrator:
   Becky Riddle
Manager of E-Commerce: Robert Young

BUSINESS STAFF

President and Chief Executive Officer:
   Rick Barton
Vice President of Sales: Mike Behar
Director of Finance and Administration:
   Laticia Mull Dittrich
Director of Corporate Planning: Anne Martin
National Sales Director: Martha Adams
Creative Services: Chaska Lucas
Information Technology Director:
   Hermine Linz
Controller: Francis Caple
Vice President, Operations: Jim Dittrich
Retail Customer Service Manager: Stan Raynor
Print Production Manager: Fred F. Pruss

We have made every effort to ensure that these instructions
are accurate and complete. We cannot, however, be
responsible for human error, typographical mistakes, or
variations in individual work.

Copyright © 2012 by Leisure Arts, Inc., 5701 Ranch Drive,
Little Rock, AR 72223. All rights reserved. This publication
is protected under federal copyright laws. Reproduction
or distribution of this publication or any other Leisure
Arts publication, including publications which are out
of print, is prohibited unless specifically authorized. This
includes, but is not limited to, any form of reproduction or
distribution on or through the Internet, including posting,
scanning, or e-mail transmission.

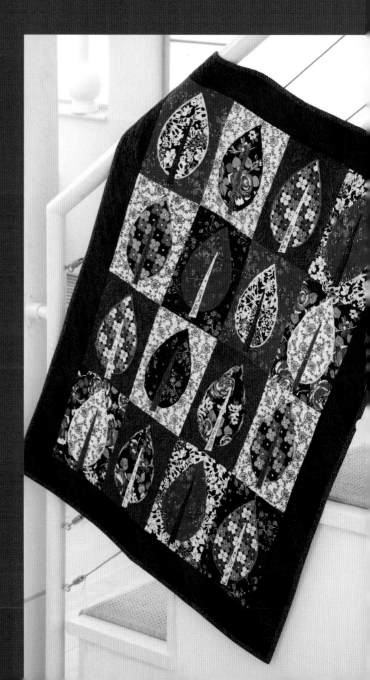

table of contents

If you like bold appliqués or fast-paced piecing—or both— you'll adore capturing the big-city style of these contemporary quilts! Start with savvy little creations like Akimbo, Papillons, and Bryant Park. Or show off cutting-edge fabrics with Cosmo Girl, Flower Power, and La Costa Del Sol. Wherever you live, there's a metropolitan pattern in this collection that's perfect for your home's décor.

Nancy Rink

A few years ago, Nancy Rink's husband Oliver spotted an ad for a national quilt design contest. He told Nancy she should enter a quilt.

Nancy, who had quilted for years from existing patterns, said, "I don't design quilts."

Oliver replied, "But you could."

She decided to give it a try—and designed a quilt that won the contest!

Since then, Nancy has won numerous awards for her designs, while her amazing quilts have appeared in several popular quilting magazines. She also works with Marcus Fabrics as a quilting consultant, designing patterns for their website and testing their new lines to see how they work in quilts. "Their fabrics are beautiful," Nancy says. "Sometimes I get to make small suggestions, such as adding one more background fabric or another fabric that pulls all the colors together."

When she isn't holding trunk shows or leading workshops, Nancy enjoys spending time with her husband, family, and dog. She also likes to read and enjoys getting together with quilting friends to sew. About six to eight times per year, she and Oliver vend at California quilt shows.

Nancy says, "My grandmother taught me to sew when I was ten or eleven. We would go to the 'yard-goods store' for fabric. When I was grown, we took a quilting class together. Grandma couldn't stand 'cutting up perfectly good fabric and sewing it back together,' but I love it! I made quilts all through the years my children were growing up.

"With modern designs like the ones in this collection, I feel free to combine traditional piecing with fusible appliqué or to add unexpected elements like buttons. Contemporary quilts are a chance to explore design options and let the fabrics tell you what they want to be. For instance, a lot of new fabrics feature larger prints. I find that simpler, cleaner designs highlight those fabrics best."

Nancy blogs at NancyRinkDesigns.blogspot.com and sells a wide variety of quilting supplies, as well as her beautiful patterns, at NancyRinkDesigns.com. She also loves to hear from quilters on her Facebook page.

akimbo

Finished Throw Size: 55" x 69" (140 cm x 175 cm)
Finished Block Size: 7^1/$_4$" x 7^1/$_4$" (18 cm x 18 cm)

yardage requirements

Yardage is based on 43"/44" (109 cm/112 cm) wide fabric with a usable width of 40" (102 cm).

- ^{3}/$_8$ yd (34 cm) *each* of 10 assorted print fabrics **or** 1 jelly roll
- 2^3/$_4$ yds (2.5 m) of black dot print fabric
- 4^3/$_8$ yds (4 m) of fabric for backing

You will also need:

- 63" x 77" (160 cm x 196 cm) piece of batting

cutting the pieces

*Follow **Rotary Cutting**, page 84, to cut fabric. Cut all strips across the selvage-to-selvage width of the fabric. Borders include extra length for "insurance" and will be trimmed after assembling quilt top center. All measurements include ^{1}/$_4$" seam allowances.*

From *each* assorted fabric:

- Cut 4 **strips** 2^1/$_2$"w.

From black dot fabric:

- Cut 18 strips 2"w. From these strips, cut 70 rectangles 2" x 9". Stack a few rectangles at a time, right side up. Refer to **Fig. 1** to cut rectangles in half once diagonally. This will yield 140 **right triangles**.

Fig. 1

- Cut 2 *lengthwise* **side inner borders** 5^3/$_8$" x 55^1/$_4$".
- Cut 2 *lengthwise* **top/bottom inner borders** 5^1/$_8$" x 50^1/$_2$".

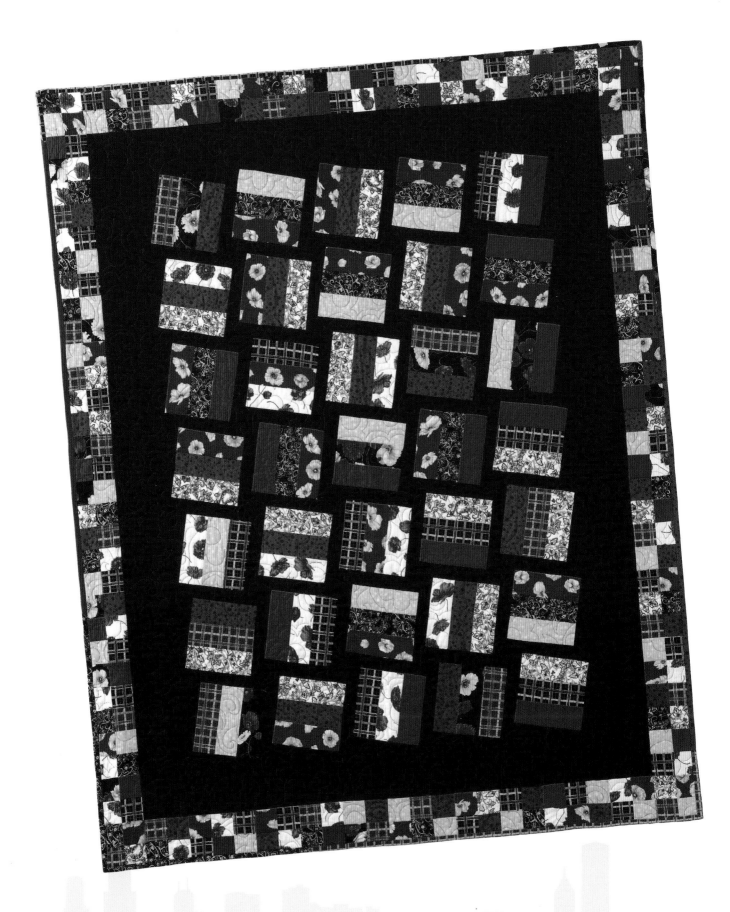

assembling the quilt top center

*Follow **Machine Piecing** and **Pressing**, page 85. Use a $1/4$" seam allowance.*

1. Sew 3 **strips** together to make **Strip Set A**. Press seam allowances in 1 direction. Make 6 Strip Set A's. Cut across Strip Set A's at $6^1/2$" intervals to make 35 **Unit 1's**.
2. Matching right sides and aligning right angle of triangle with corner of Unit 1, pin a **right triangle** to 1 edge of a Unit 1. Referring to **Block Assembly Diagram**, begin sewing the seam in the area indicated by the yellow dot. Press the seam allowances toward the right triangle.
3. Rotate Unit 1 counter-clockwise and add another right triangle, this time sewing the entire length of the seam. Repeat, sewing a right triangle to each side of Unit 1 to make a **Block**. After you have added the fourth triangle, finish the seam on the first triangle.
4. Repeat Steps 2-3 to make 35 Blocks. Trim each Block to $7^3/4$" x $7^3/4$".
5. Referring to **Quilt Top Diagram**, page 10, and rotating the Blocks as desired, lay out the Blocks. Sew 5 Blocks together to make a **Row**. Make 7 Rows.
6. Sew Rows together to make Quilt Top Center. Quilt Top Center should now measure $36^3/4$" x $51^1/4$" including seam allowances.

adding the borders

1. Follow **Adding Squared Borders**, page 88, to add **side**, then **top** and **bottom inner borders**. Quilt top should now measure $46^1/2$" x $60^1/2$" including seam allowances.
2. Sew 2 **strips** together to make **Strip Set B**. Press seam allowances in 1 direction. Make 8 Strip Set B's. Cut across Strip Set B's at $2^1/2$" intervals to make 114 **Unit 2's**. Set aside remaining portion of Strip Set B.
3. Sew 23 Unit 2's together to make **top outer border**. Finger-press as you go to alternate direction of seam allowances. Repeat to make **bottom outer border**.
4. Matching centers and corners, sew top and bottom outer borders to quilt top. Press seam allowances toward inner borders.

5. Sew 34 Unit 2's together to make **side outer border**. Finger-press as you go to alternate direction of seam allowances. Pay attention to fabric placement at the corners so that darks and lights alternate. Repeat to make another side outer border.
6. Matching centers and corners, sew side outer borders to quilt top. Press seam allowances toward inner border.

Strip Set A (make 6)   **Unit 1** (make 35)

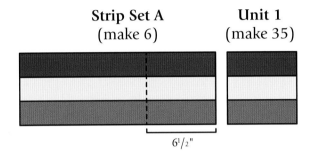

$6^1/2$"

Block Assembly Diagram

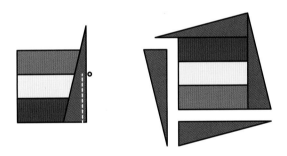

Block (make 35)

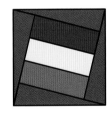

Strip Set B (make 8)   **Unit 2** (make 114)

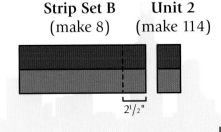

$2^1/2$"

finishing the quilt

Fig. 2

1. Stay-stitch around the outside edge of the quilt top to keep seams from opening during quilting.
2. Follow **Quilting**, page 90, to mark, layer, and quilt. Our quilt is machine quilted with an all-over meandering pattern using red thread.
3. Sew remaining **strips** together using a diagonal seam (**Fig. 2**) to make a continuous binding strip. If additional length is needed, remove seams from leftover Strip Set B set aside earlier and use these strips.
4. Follow **Attaching Binding with Mitered Corners**, page 94, to bind quilt.

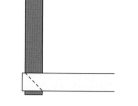

Quilt Top Diagram

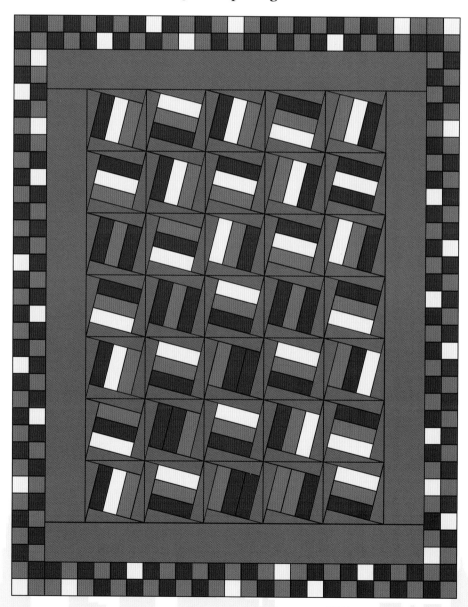

	Twin Size: 71" x 85" (180 cm x 216 cm)	King Size: 93" x 93" (236 cm x 236 cm)
Finished Size	Twin Size: 71" x 85" (180 cm x 216 cm)	King Size: 93" x 93" (236 cm x 236 cm)
Blocks	Block Size: $7^1/4$" x $7^1/4$" (18 cm x 18 cm) Block Layout: 63 (7 x 9)	Block Size: $7^1/4$" x $7^1/4$" (18 cm x 18 cm) Block Layout: 100 (10 x 10)
Fabric Requirements	$5/8$ yd (57 cm) *each* of 10 assorted print fabrics 4 yds (3.7 m) of black dot print fabric $5^1/4$ yds (4.8 m) of fabric for backing	$7/8$ yd (80 cm) *each* of 10 assorted print fabrics $5^5/8$ yds (5.1 m) of black dot print fabric $8^1/2$ yds (7.8 m) of fabric for backing
You will also need	79" x 93" (201 cm x 236 cm) piece of batting	101" x 101" (257 cm x 257 cm) piece of batting
Cut pieces	**From assorted print fabrics:** Cut a *total* of 33 strips $2^1/2$"w for blocks. Make 11 Strip Set A's and cut 63 Unit 1's. Cut a *total* of 20 strips $2^1/2$"w for outer border. Make 10 Strip Set B's and cut 146 Unit 2's. Cut 9 **binding strips** $2^1/2$"w. **From black dot print fabric:** Cut 32 strips 2"w. From these strips, cut 126 rectangles 2" x 9". Stack a few rectangles at a time, right side up. Cut rectangles in half once diagonally to make 252 **right triangles.** Cut 2 *lengthwise* **side inner borders** $6^1/8$" x $69^3/4$". Cut 2 *lengthwise* **top/bottom inner borders** $5^7/8$" x $66^1/2$".	**From assorted print fabrics:** Cut a *total* of 51 strips $2^1/2$"w for blocks. Make 17 Strip Set A's and cut 100 Unit 1's. Cut a *total* of 22 strips $2^1/2$"w for outer border. Make 11 Strip Set B's and cut 176 Unit 2's. Cut 11 **binding strips** $2^1/2$"w. **From black dot print fabric:** Cut 50 strips 2"w. From these strips, cut 200 rectangles 2" x 9". Stack a few rectangles at a time, right side up. Cut rectangles in half once diagonally to make 400 **right triangles.** Cut 2 *lengthwise* **side inner borders** $6^1/4$" x 77". Cut 2 *lengthwise* **top/bottom inner borders** $6^1/4$" x $88^1/2$".

bryant park

Finished Wall Hanging Size: 29" x 33" (74 cm x 84 cm)

yardage requirements

Yardage is based on 43"/44" (109 cm/112 cm) wide fabric with a usable width of 40" (102 cm). A fat quarter measures approximately 21" x 18" (53 cm x 46 cm).

> 1 fat quarter *each* of 6 assorted pink print *or* blue print fabrics
> 1 fat quarter of ivory tone-on-tone print fabric
> 1 yd (91 cm) of brown tone-on-tone print fabric
> 1¼ yds (1.1 m) of fabric for backing
> ⅜ yd (34 cm) of fabric for binding

You will also need:

> 37" x 41" (94 cm x 104 cm) piece of batting
> Paper-backed fusible web
> Stabilizer

cutting the pieces

*Follow **Rotary Cutting**, page 84, to cut fabric. Cut all strips across the selvage-to-selvage width of the fabric. All measurements include ¼" seam allowances.*

From assorted pink print *or* blue print fabrics:
- Cut a *total* of 17 **strips** 2½" x 21".
- Cut 4 **inner corner squares** 3½" x 3½".

From ivory tone-on-tone print fabric:
- Cut **background** 10½" x 14½".

From brown tone-on-tone print fabric:
- Cut 4 **top/bottom sashings** 2" x 16½".
- Cut 4 **side sashings** 2" x 20½".
- Cut 4 **outer corner squares** 7½" x 7½".

From fabric for binding:
- Cut 4 **binding strips** 2¼"w.

cutting the appliqués

*Follow **Preparing Fusible Appliqués**, page 87, to use patterns, pages 20, 22, and 23. **Note:** Appliqué patterns are printed in reverse.*

From assorted pink print *or* blue print fabrics:
- Cut 32 **flower petals V**.
- Cut 4 **flower centers W**.

From brown tone-on-tone print fabric:
- Cut 1 *each* of appliqués **A - U**.

Nancy made her beautiful wall hanging in both a blue version, shown here, and a pink version, page 14.

assembling the background

*Follow **Machine Piecing** and **Pressing**, page 85. Use a $^1/_4$" seam allowance.*

1. Sew 7 assorted **strips** together to make **Strip Set A**. Press seam allowances in 1 direction. Cut across Strip Set A at $3^1/_2$" intervals to make 4 **inner borders**.

2. Sew 1 inner border to each side of the **background**. Press seam allowances open.

3. Remove 1 piece from each end of the remaining inner borders. Sew 1 **inner corner square** to ends of each remaining inner border. Press seam allowances open. Sew inner border to top and bottom of background. Press seam allowances open.

Strip Set A   **Inner Borders**
                    (make 4)

$3^1/_2$"

adding the appliqués

1. Arrange and fuse appliqués **A - U** to background and inner borders. Follow **Satin Stitch Appliqué**, page 87, to stitch appliqués in place.
2. Arrange and fuse appliqués **V - W** on **outer corner squares**. Satin Stitch appliqués in place. Trim outer corner squares to $6^1/_2$" x $6^1/_2$"; set aside.

adding the borders

1. Sew 10 assorted **strips** together to make **Strip Set B**. Press seam allowances in 1 direction. Cut across Strip Set B at $3^1/_2$" intervals to make 4 **Outer Border Units**.
2. Sew 1 **side sashing** to each side of 1 Outer Border Unit to make a **Side Outer Border**. Press seam allowances toward the brown fabric. Make 2 Side Outer Borders.
3. Remove 1 piece from each end of each remaining border unit.
4. Sew 1 **top/bottom sashing** to each side of 1 border unit to make top/bottom outer border. Press seam allowances toward the brown fabric. Make 2 top/bottom outer borders.
5. Sew 1 side outer border to each side of wall hanging top. Press seam allowances toward the outer border.
6. Sew 1 outer corner square to each end of 1 top/bottom outer border. Repeat with remaining top/bottom outer border.
7. Sew top and bottom outer borders to wall hanging top. Press seam allowances toward the outer border.

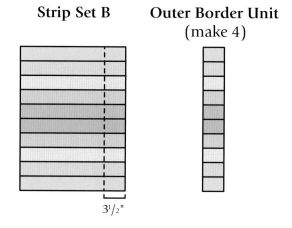

Strip Set B   **Outer Border Unit** (make 4)

$3^1/_2$"

Side Outer Border (make 2)

Top/Bottom Outer Border (make 2)

finishing the quilt

1. Follow **Quilting**, page 90, to mark, layer, and quilt. Both versions of our wall hanging are machine quilted in the ditch along the borders and sashings.

   The blue version is quilted with wavy lines in each inner sashing and in the large flower petals. There are curlicues stitched in the leaves and between the petals in the outer corner squares. There are meandering swirls on the remainder of the quilt top.

   For the pink version, the outer corner squares have a square quilted behind the petals. The square is filled with stipple quilting. There are meandering swirls on the remainder of the quilt top.

2. Refer to **Making a Hanging Sleeve,** page 92, if a hanging sleeve is desired.

3. Sew **binding strips** together using diagonal seams (**Fig. 1**) to make a continuous binding strip. Follow **Attaching Binding with Mitered Corners**, page 94, to bind quilt.

Wall Hanging Top Diagram

Fig. 1

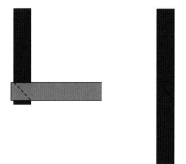

Alternate Sizes

	Throw Size (shown on page 20): 55" x 63" (140 cm x 160 cm)	Twin Size (shown on page 21): 73" x 85" (185 cm x 216 cm)
Finished Size		
Blocks	**Block Size:** 16" x 20" (41 cm x 51 cm) **Corner Square Size:** 6" x 6" (15 cm x 15 cm) **Block Layout:** 4 (2 x 2)	**Block Size:** 16" x 20" (41 cm x 51 cm) **Corner Square Size:** 6" x 6" (15 cm x 15 cm) **Block Layout:** 9 (3 x 3)
Fabric Requirements	1 fat quarter *each* of 6 assorted pink prints and 6 assorted blue prints 1 fat quarter of blue tone-on-tone print fabric $1^3/8$ yds (1.3 m) of ivory tone-on-tone print fabric $1^3/4$ yds (1.6 m) of brown tone-on-tone print fabric 4 yds (3.7 m) of fabric for backing $^1/2$ yd (46 cm) of fabric for binding	1 fat quarter *each* of 10 assorted pink prints and 10 assorted blue prints 1 fat quarter of blue tone-on-tone print fabric $2^1/4$ yds (2.1 m) of ivory tone-on-tone print fabric $3^1/2$ yds (3.2 m) of brown tone-on-tone print fabric $6^3/4$ yds (6.2 m) of fabric for backing $^5/8$ yd (57 cm) of fabric for binding
You will also need	63" x 71" (160 cm x 180 cm) piece of batting	81" x 93" (206 cm x 236 cm) piece of batting
Cut pieces	**From assorted blue print fat quarters:** Cut a *total* of 14 strips $2^1/2$" x 21" for blocks. Make 2 Strip Set A's of 7 strips each and cut 8 Inner Borders. Remove rectangles as needed for borders. Cut a *total* of 11 strips $2^1/2$" x 21" for outer borders. Make 1 Strip Set B of 11 strips and cut 4 Outer Border Units. Remove rectangles as needed for borders. Cut 8 **inner corner squares** $3^1/2$" x $3^1/2$". **From assorted pink print fat quarters:** Cut a *total* of 14 strips $2^1/2$" x 21" for blocks. Make 2 Strip Set A's of 7 strips each and cut 8 Inner Borders. Remove rectangles as needed for borders. Cut a *total* of 12 strips $2^1/2$" x 21" for outer borders. Make 1 Strip Set B of 12 strips and cut 4 Outer Border Units. Remove rectangles as needed for borders. Cut 8 **inner corner squares** $3^1/2$" x $3^1/2$".	**From assorted blue print fat quarters:** Cut a *total* of 28 strips $2^1/2$" x 21" for blocks. Make 4 Strip Set A's of 7 strips each and cut 20 Inner Borders. Remove rectangles as needed for borders. Cut a *total* of 17 strips $2^1/2$" x 21" for borders. Make 1 Strip Set B and cut 4 Outer Border Units. Remove rectangles as needed for borders. Cut 20 **inner corner squares** $3^1/2$" x $3^1/2$". **From assorted pink print fat quarters:** Cut a *total* of 21 strips $2^1/2$" x 21" for blocks. Make 3 Strip Set A's of 7 strips each and cut 16 Inner Borders. Remove rectangles as needed for borders. Cut a *total* of 17 strips $2^1/2$" x 21" for outer borders. Make 1 Strip Set B and cut 4 Outer Border Units. Remove rectangles as needed for borders. Cut 16 **inner corner squares** $3^1/2$" x $3^1/2$".

Cut pieces (cont.)	**From blue tone-on-tone fat quarter:** Cut 2 strips $2^1/_2$" x 21". From these strips, cut 9 **sashing squares** $2^1/_2$" x $2^1/_2$". **From ivory tone-on-tone print fabric:** Cut 2 strips $14^1/_2$"w. From these strips, cut 4 **backgrounds** $10^1/_2$" x $14^1/_2$". Cut 6 strips $2^1/_2$"w. From *each* strip, cut 1 **vertical sashing strip** $2^1/_2$" x $20^1/_2$" and 1 **horizontal sashing strip** $2^1/_2$" x $16^1/_2$". **From brown tone-on-tone print fabric:** Cut 4 **top/bottom sashings** 2" x $38^1/_2$". Cut 4 **side sashings** 2" x $46^1/_2$", pieced as needed. Cut 1 strip $7^1/_2$"w. From this strip, cut 4 **outer corner squares** $7^1/_2$" x $7^1/_2$". Cut 2 **top/bottom outermost borders** $2^1/_2$" x $54^1/_2$", pieced as needed. Cut 2 **side outermost borders** $2^1/_2$" x $58^1/_2$", pieced as needed. **From fabric for binding:** Cut 7 **binding strips** $2^1/_4$"w.	**From blue tone-on-tone fat quarter:** Cut 2 strips $2^1/_2$" x 21". From these strips, cut 16 **sashing squares** $2^1/_2$" x $2^1/_2$". **From ivory tone-on-tone print fabric:** Cut 3 strips $14^1/_2$"w. From these strips, cut 9 **backgrounds** $10^1/_2$" x $14^1/_2$". Cut 12 strips $2^1/_2$"w. From *each* strip, cut 1 **vertical sashing strip** $2^1/_2$" x $20^1/_2$" and 1 **horizontal sashing strip** $2^1/_2$" x $16^1/_2$". **From brown tone-on-tone print fabric:** Cut 4 **top/bottom sashings** 2" x $56^1/_2$", pieced as needed. Cut 4 **side sashings** 2" x $68^1/_2$", pieced as needed. Cut 1 strip $7^1/_2$"w. From this strip, cut 4 **outer corner squares** $7^1/_2$" x $7^1/_2$". Cut 2 **top/bottom outermost borders** $2^1/_2$" x $72^1/_2$", pieced as needed. Cut 2 **side outermost borders** $2^1/_2$" x $80^1/_2$", pieced as needed. **From fabric for binding:** Cut 9 **binding strips** $2^1/_4$"w.
Cut appliqué pieces	**From assorted blue print fabrics:** Cut 16 **flower petals V.** Cut 2 **flower centers W.** **From assorted pink print fabrics:** Cut 16 **flower petals V.** Cut 2 **flower centers W.** **From brown tone-on-tone print fabric:** Cut 4 *each* of appliqués **A-U.**	**From assorted blue print fabrics:** Cut 16 **flower petals V.** Cut 2 **flower centers W.** **From assorted pink print fabrics:** Cut 16 **flower petals V.** Cut 2 **flower centers W.** **From brown tone-on-tone print fabric:** Cut 9 *each* of appliqués **A-U.**

Throw Quilt Top Diagram

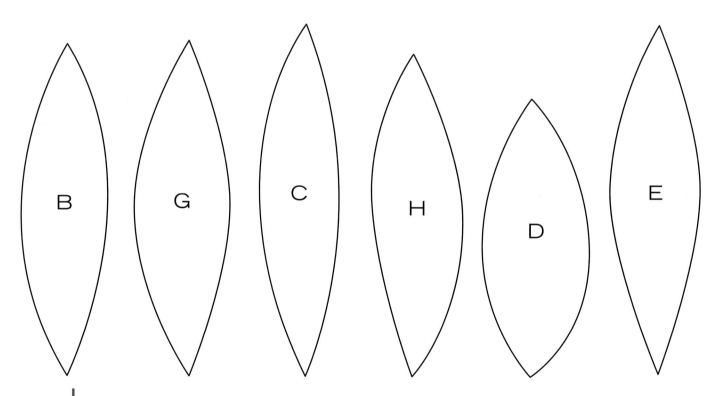

Twin Quilt Top Diagram

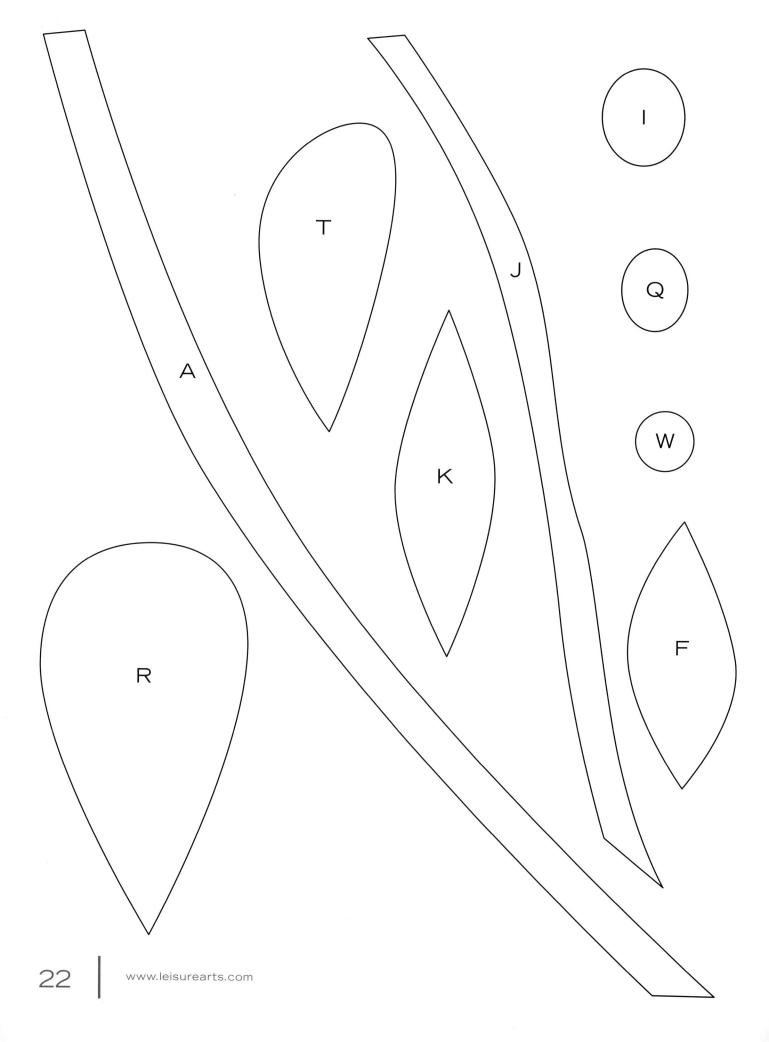

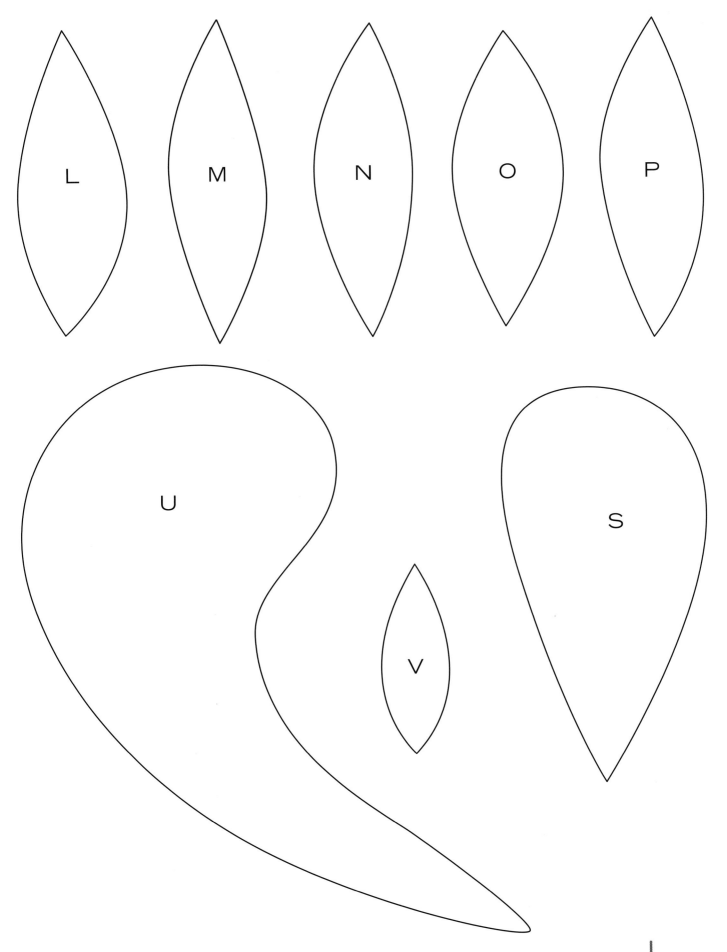

cosmo girl

Finished Throw Size: 41" x 51" (104 cm x 130 cm)
Finished Block Size: 9" x 12" (23 cm x 30 cm)

yardage requirements

Yardage is based on 42"/43" (109 cm/112 cm) wide fabric with a usable width of 40" (102 cm).

- 1 yd (91 cm) of brown and aqua print fabric
- 1 yd (91 cm) of aqua print fabric
- 1 yd (91 cm) of lime green print fabric
- ⁷/₈ yd (80 cm) of pale aqua print fabric
- ⁵/₈ yd (57 cm) of pale pink print fabric
- ¹/₂ yd (46 cm) of brown and pink print fabric
- ¹/₂ yd (46 cm) of hot pink print fabric
- ¹/₂ yd (46 cm) of multi-color large print fabric
- 3³/₈ yds (3.1 m) of fabric for backing

You will also need:

- 49" x 59" (124 cm x 150 cm) piece of batting
- Paper-backed fusible web
- Stabilizer

cutting the pieces

*Follow **Rotary Cutting**, page 84, to cut fabric. Cut all strips across the selvage-to-selvage width of the fabric. All measurements include ¹/₄" seam allowances.*

From brown and aqua print fabric:
- Cut 6 **binding strips** 2¹/₂"w.

From aqua print fabric:
- Cut 2 **side outer borders** 5¹/₂" x 40¹/₂"; pieced as needed.
- Cut 2 **top/bottom outer borders** 5¹/₂" x 30¹/₂".

From lime green print fabric:
- Cut 2 **strips for top/bottom scallops** 2¹/₂" x 30¹/₂".
- Cut 2 **strips for side scallops** 2¹/₂" x 40¹/₂"; pieced as needed.
- Cut 2 **side inner borders** 1¹/₂" x 36¹/₂".
- Cut 2 **top/bottom inner borders** 2" x 29¹/₂".
- Cut 1 strip 6¹/₂"w. From this strip, cut 4 **border corners** 6¹/₂" x 6¹/₂".

From pale aqua print fabric:
- Cut 2 strips 13" wide. From these strips, cut 6 **large rectangles** 10" x 13".

From pale pink print fabric:
- Cut 1 **large rectangle** 10" x 13".
- Cut 4 **small rectangles** 9¹/₂" x 6¹/₂".

From brown and pink print fabric:
- Cut 2 **side middle borders** 1" x 39¹/₂".
- Cut 2 **top/bottom middle borders** 1" x 30¹/₂".

cutting the appliqués

*Follow **Preparing Fusible Appliqués**, page 87, to use patterns, pages 29 - 31. **Note:** Appliqué patterns are printed in reverse.*

From brown and aqua print fabric:
- Cut 4 **flowers B**.
- Cut 4 **outer centers E**.
- Cut 4 **outer leaves G**.
- Cut 4 **outer leaves I**.
- Cut 2 **large circles L**.

From aqua print fabric:
- Cut 7 **stems A**.
- Cut 2 **flowers C**.
- Cut 1 **flower D**.
- Cut 2 **medium circles M**.

From lime green print fabric:
- Cut 2 **flowers C**.
- Cut 2 **flowers D**.
- Cut 2 strips of fusible web $2^1/2$" x $40^1/2$". For each scallop appliqué, trace scallop pattern, page 29, end to end, 4 times, onto fusible web. Fuse web to wrong side of strips for side scallops. Cut 2 **side scallops**.
- Cut 2 strips of fusible web $2^1/2$" x $30^1/2$". For each scallop appliqué, trace scallop pattern, page 29, end to end, 3 times, onto fusible web. Fuse web to wrong side of strips for top/bottom scallops. Cut 2 **top/bottom scallops**.

From pale aqua print fabric:
- Cut 2 **flowers N**.

From pale pink print fabric:
- Cut 2 **flowers D**.
- Cut 2 **flowers N**.

From brown and pink print fabric:
- Cut 3 **flowers B**.
- Cut 3 **outer centers E**.
- Cut 3 **outer leaves G**.
- Cut 3 **outer leaves I**.
- Cut 2 **large circles L**.

From hot pink print fabric:
- Cut 2 **flowers C**.
- Cut 2 **flowers D**.
- Cut 2 **medium circles M**.
- Cut 77 **small circles K**.

From multi-colored large print fabric:
- Cut 1 **flowers C**.
- Cut 7 **centers F**.
- Cut 7 **inner leaves H**.
- Cut 7 **inner leaves J**.
- Cut 4 **very small circles O**.

making the appliqué blocks

1. Arrange and fuse appliqués **A – K** to pale aqua and pale pink **large rectangles**.
2. Arrange and fuse **side scallops** to 1 edge of **side outer border** and **top/bottom scallops** to 1 edge of **top/bottom outer borders**. Fuse remaining small circles K to scallops.
3. Arrange and fuse 1 *each* of **L**, **M**, **N**, and **O** to each **border corner**.
4. Follow **Satin Stitch Appliqué**, page 87, to stitch appliqués in place. Press from the wrong side of the block. Trim large rectangles to $9^1/2$" x $12^1/2$" to make Appliqué Blocks. Trim border corners to $5^1/2$" x $5^1/2$".

assembling the quilt top

*Follow **Machine Piecing** and **Pressing**, page 85, to assemble the quilt top. Refer to **Quilt Top Diagram**, page 28, for placement.*

1. Lay out Appliqué Blocks and **small rectangles** as shown. Sew pieces together in vertical rows. Sew rows together to make quilt top center. Quilt Top Center should measure $27^1/2$" x $36^1/2$" including seam allowances.
2. Matching centers and corners, sew 1 **side inner border** to opposite sides of quilt top center. Press seam allowances toward inner border.
3. Sew **top** and **bottom inner borders** to quilt top center. Press seam allowances toward border.
4. Sew 1 **side middle border** to opposite sides of quilt top. Press seam allowances toward inner border.
5. Sew **top** and **bottom middle borders** to quilt top. Press seam allowances toward inner border.
6. Sew 1 **side outer border** to opposite sides of quilt top. Press seam allowances toward middle border.
7. Sew 1 border corner to ends of each **top/bottom outer border**. Sew top and bottom outer borders to quilt top. Press seam allowances toward middle border.

completing the quilt

Fig. 1

1. Follow **Quilting**, page 90, to mark, layer, and quilt as desired. Quilt shown is machine quilted in the ditch along the middle border, around the scallops, and around the flowers in the border corners. There is an all-over feather pattern quilted in the background and borders. The border corners have a meandering swirl pattern around the large circle.

2. Sew **binding strips** together end to end using diagonal seams (**Fig. 1**) to make a continuous binding strip.

3. Follow **Attaching Binding With Mitered Corners**, page 94, to bind quilt.

Quilt Top Diagram

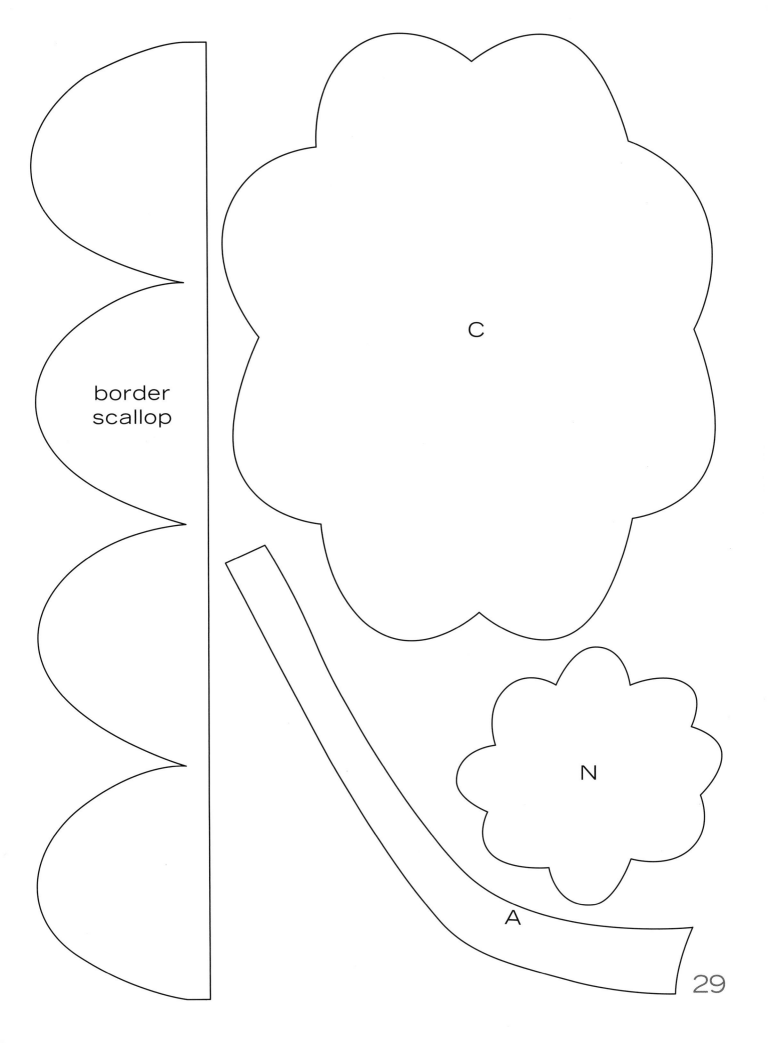

border
scallop

C

N

A

29

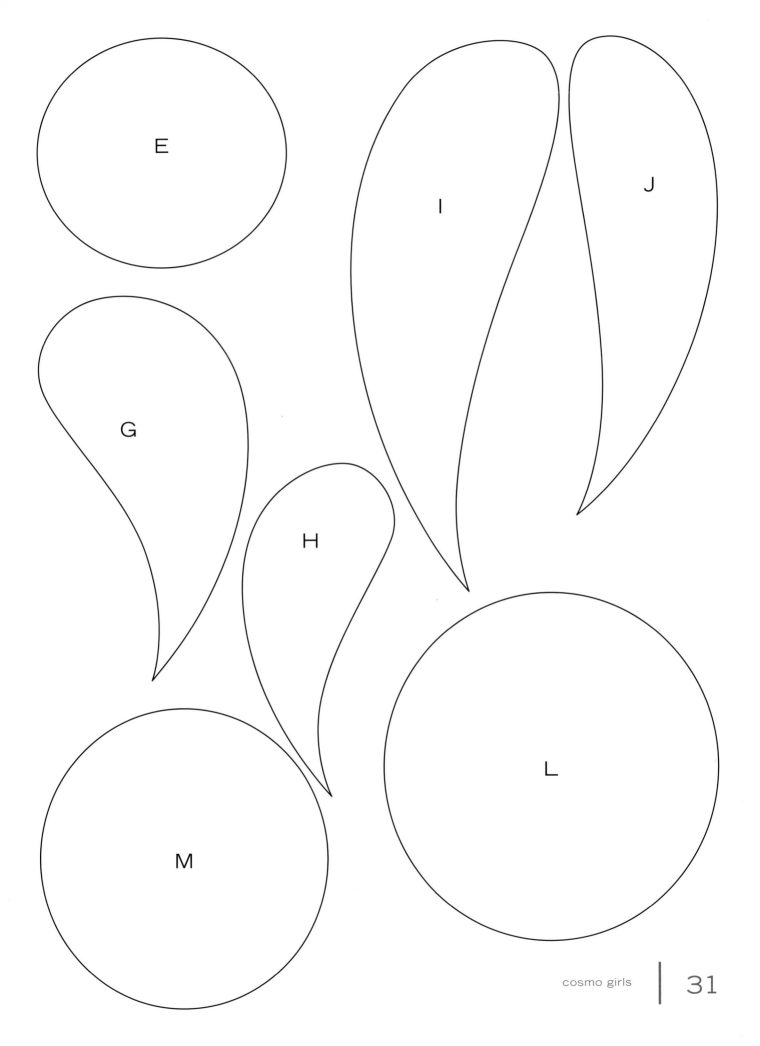

E

I

J

G

H

L

M

espresso

Finished Quilt Size: 73" x 85" (185 cm x 216 cm)
Finished Block Size: 9" x 9" (23 cm x 23 cm)

yardage requirements

Yardage is based on 42"/43" (109 cm/112 cm) wide fabric with a usable width of 40" (102 cm).

- 5³/₄ yds (5.3 m) of chocolate brown solid fabric
- 14 fat quarters **or** a ***total*** of 3¹/₂ yds (3.2 m) of assorted pink, red, brown, and green print fabrics
- 6³/₄ yds (6.2 m) of fabric for backing

You will also need:

- 81" x 93" (206 cm x 236 cm) piece of batting
- 9 yds (8.2 m) of 1 mm – 5 mm polyester or nylon cord for piping
- Template plastic

cutting the pieces

*Follow **Rotary Cutting**, page 84, to cut fabric. Cut all strips across the selvage-to-selvage width of the fabric unless otherwise indicated. Borders include extra length for "insurance" and will be trimmed after assembling quilt top center. All measurements include ¹/₄" seam allowances.*

From chocolate brown solid fabric:

- Cut 13 strips 2¹/₂"w. From these strips, cut 200 **squares A** 2¹/₂" x 2¹/₂".
- Cut 1 strip 3¹/₂". From this strip, cut 4 **squares B** 3¹/₂" x 3¹/₂".
- Cut 4 strips 4"w. From these strips, cut 38 **squares C** 4" x 4".
- Cut 13 strips 3¹/₂"w. From these strips, cut 49 **sashings** 3¹/₂" x 9¹/₂".
- Cut 9 **binding strips** 2"w.
- Cut 2 *lengthwise* **side outer borders** 8" x 73¹/₂".
- Cut 2 *lengthwise* **top/bottom outer borders** 8" x 76¹/₂".

From assorted pink, red, brown, and green print fabrics:

- Cut 100 sets of 2 matching **squares A** 2¹/₂" x 2¹/₂".
- Cut 20 sets of 4 matching **squares B** 3¹/₂" x 3¹/₂".
- Cut 38 **squares C** 4" x 4".
- Cut 30 **sashing squares D** 3¹/₂" x 3¹/₂".
- Cut 17 **piping strips** 1" x 21".

cutting the appliqués

*Follow **Making and Using Templates**, page 86, to make templates for each appliqué piece using patterns, page 39.*

From assorted pink, red, brown, and green print fabrics:

- Cut 8 **stems** using template **E**.
- Cut 16 **flower petals** using template **F**.
- Cut 48 **leaves** using template **G**.
- Cut 8 **leaves** using template **H**.
- Cut 2 **flower centers** using template **I**.

making the triangle-squares

*Follow **Machine Piecing** and **Pressing**, page 85, to assemble the quilt top.*

1. Draw a diagonal line on wrong side of each assorted pink, red, brown, and green print fabric **square A**. With right sides together, place 1 assorted square A on top of 1 brown **square A**. Stitch ¹/₄" from each side of drawn line (**Fig. 1**).

2. Cut along drawn line and press seam allowances toward the brown fabric to make 2 **Triangle-Square A's**. Make 400 Triangle-Square A's. Trim each Triangle-Square A to 2" x 2".

3. Draw a diagonal line on wrong side of each assorted pink, red, brown, and green print fabric **square C**. With right sides together, place 1 assorted square C on top of 1 brown **square C**. Stitch ¹/₄" from each side of drawn line (**Fig. 2**).

4. Cut along drawn line and press seam allowances toward the brown fabric to make 2 **Triangle-Square B's**. Make 76 Triangle-Square B's. Trim each Triangle-Square B to 3¹/₂" x 3¹/₂".

Fig. 1

Triangle-Square A (make 400)

Fig. 2

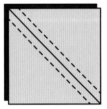

Triangle-Square B (make 76)

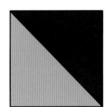

making the blocks

1. For each Block, select 5 sets of 4 matching Triangle-Square A's and 4 matching assorted **square B's**.
2. Sew 4 matching Triangle-Square A's together to make a **Pinwheel Unit**. Make 100 Pinwheel Units.
3. Sew 2 Pinwheel Units and 1 **square B** together to make **Row A**. Make 2 Row A's.
4. Sew 2 square B's and 1 Pinwheel Unit together to make **Row B**.
5. Sew Rows A and B together to make a **Block**. Repeat Steps 1-4 to make 20 Blocks.

assembling the quilt top

Follow **Needle-Turn Appliqué**, *page 86, and refer to* **Quilt Assembly Diagram**, *page 38, for placement.*

1. Sew 4 Blocks and 5 **sashings** together to make a **Block Row**. Make 5 Block Rows.
2. Sew 4 sashings and 5 **sashing square D's** together to make **Sashing Row**. Make 6 Sashing Rows.
3. Sew Block Rows and Sashing Rows together to make quilt top center.
4. Sew 21 **Triangle-Square B's** together to make **side inner border**. Make 2 side inner borders.
5. Sew 17 **Triangle-Square B's** together to make **top inner border**. Repeat to make **bottom inner border**.
6. Matching centers and corners, sew 1 side inner border to each side of quilt top center. Press seam allowances toward quilt top center.
7. Sew 1 brown **square B** to each end of top inner border. Repeat for bottom inner border.
8. Sew top and bottom inner borders to quilt top center. Press seam allowances toward the quilt top center.
9. Measure length through center of quilt top to determine length of side outer borders. Trim **side outer borders** to determined length.

Pinwheel Unit (make 100)

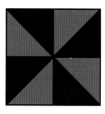

Row A (make 2)

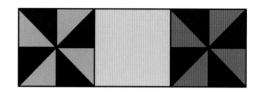

Row B

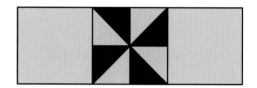

Block (make 20)

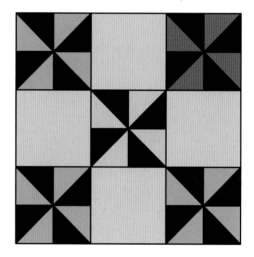

10. Arrange appliqués **E** and **G – I** on side outer borders. Pin all pieces in place. Appliqué each piece to borders starting with lowest layers and working to top layers.
11. Sew 1 side outer border to each side of quilt top.
12. Measure width through center of quilt top to determine length of top/bottom outer borders. Trim **top** and **bottom outer borders** to determined length.
13. Arrange appliqués **E – I** on top and bottom outer borders. You will need to leave the end of at least 1 flower petal loose because it overlaps the stem on the adjoining border.
14. Sew top outer border and bottom outer border to quilt top.
15. Appliqué end of loose flower petals in place.

completing the quilt

1. Follow **Quilting**, page 90, to mark, layer, and quilt as desired. Quilt shown is machine quilted in the ditch around all blocks. Each pinwheel unit has curved petals and each Square B has a flower. The remainder of the block is stipple quilted. Each sashing has a feather pattern and each colored triangle of the inner border has 3 petals. The outer border is quilted with a flower and leaf pattern replicating the appliqué design.
2. Sew assorted **piping strips** together end to end using a diagonal seam (**Fig. 3**) to make a continuous piping strip. Press seam allowances open. Matching wrong sides, press strip in half.

3. Tie a knot in 1 end of the cord. To make piping, lay the cord in the crease of the piping strip. Attach a zipper foot or piping foot to sewing machine. With seam allowance to the right and the edge of the foot against the cord, stitch next to the cord. Stitch the entire length of the piping strip.
4. Trim the seam allowance of the piping to $^{1}/_{4}$".
5. Leaving about 1" excess piping at beginning and end of each side, align the raw edge of the piping with the edge of the quilt top and sew the piping one side at a time to the quilt. When all piping is attached, trim the excess length.
6. Sew **binding strips** together end to end using diagonal seams (see **Fig. 3**) to make a continuous binding strip.
7. Follow **Attaching Binding With Mitered Corners**, page 94, to bind quilt.

Fig. 3

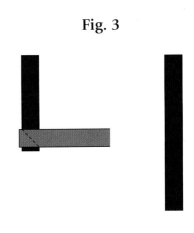

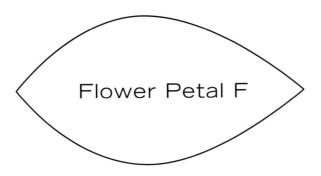

Stem E

Flower Petal F

Flower Center
I

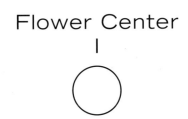

Leaf G

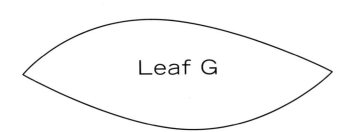

Leaf H

flower power

Finished Quilt Size: 62 " x 71 " (157 cm x 180 cm)
Finished Appliqué Block Size: 9" x 9" (23 cm x 23 cm)
Finished Hourglass Block Size: 4½" x 4½" (11 cm x 11 cm)

yardage requirements

Yardage is based on 42"/43" (109 cm/112 cm) wide fabric with a usable width of 40" (102 cm).

- ³/₈ yd (34 cm) *total* of assorted green print fabrics for stems and leaves
- ³/₈ yd (34 cm) of orange persimmon print fabric for Hourglass Blocks and appliqués
- ½ yd (46 cm) of multi-color stripe fabric for inner borders
- 2⅝ yds (2.4 m) of large floral print fabric for outer borders and Hourglass Blocks (If fabric is not directional you will need 1⅝ yds [1.5 m]).
- 1 yd (91 cm) *total* of assorted orange, gold, pink, and red-orange print fabrics for appliqués and Hourglass Blocks
- ³/₈ yd (34 cm) *total* of assorted yellow print fabrics for appliqués
- 1 yd (91 cm) *each* of 3 assorted burgundy mottled print fabrics for background
- ⁷/₈ yd (80 cm) of red-orange stripe fabric for binding
- 4½ yds (4.1 m) of fabric for backing

You will also need:

- 70" x 79" (178 cm x 201 cm) piece of batting
- Paper-backed fusible web
- Stabilizer

cutting the pieces

*Follow **Rotary Cutting**, page 84, to cut fabric. Cut all strips across the selvage-to-selvage width of the fabric. Borders include extra length for "insurance" and will be trimmed after assembling quilt top center. All measurements include ¼" seam allowances.*

From orange persimmon print fabric:

- Cut 1 strip 5⅞"w. From this strip, cut 6 squares 5⅞" x 5⅞" for Hourglass Blocks.

From multi-color stripe fabric:

- Cut 2 **top/bottom inner borders** 2½" x 53½", pieced as needed.
- Cut 2 **side inner borders** 2½" x 62½", pieced as needed.

From large floral print fabric:

- Cut 2 *crosswise* **top/bottom borders** 6½" x 65½", pieced as needed.
- Cut 2 *lengthwise* **side borders** 6½" x 62½".

From remaining width:

- Cut 6 **squares** 5⅞" x 5⅞" for Hourglass Blocks.

Continued on page 43.

cutting the pieces (cont.)

From assorted orange, gold, pink, and red-orange print fabrics:
- Cut 12 **squares** $5^7/_8$" x $5^7/_8$" for Hourglass Blocks.

From the 3 burgundy mottled print fabrics:
- Cut a *total* of 18 **background squares** $10^1/_2$" x $10^1/_2$".
- Cut a *total* of 22 **squares** $5^7/_8$" x $5^7/_8$" for Hourglass Blocks.
- Cut a *total* of 8 **squares** $3^1/_4$" x $3^1/_4$". Cut each square *once* diagonally to make 16 **small triangles** for Flying Geese.

From red-orange stripe fabric:
- Cut 1 **binding square** 27" x 27".

cutting the appliqués

Follow **Preparing Fusible Appliqués**, page 87, to use patterns, page 47. **Note:** *Appliqué patterns are printed in reverse.*

From assorted green print fabrics:
- Cut 9 **stems**.
- Cut 9 **stems in reverse**.
- Cut 18 **hearts**.
- Cut 36 **leaves**.

From orange persimmon print fabric:
- Cut 3 sets of 7 **buds in reverse**.
- Cut 3 **large flower centers**.
- Cut 3 **small flower centers**.

From assorted orange, gold, pink, and red-orange print fabrics:
- Cut 9 sets of 7 **buds**.
- Cut 6 sets of 7 **buds in reverse**.
- Cut 15 **large flower centers**.
- Cut 15 **small flower centers**.

From assorted yellow print fabrics:
- Cut 18 **flowers**.

making the flying geese

Follow **Machine Piecing** *and* **Pressing**, *page 85, to assemble the quilt top.*

1. Cut 1 *each* of the orange persimmon print and pink print squares *twice* diagonally to make 8 **large triangles**.
2. Sew 1 orange persimmon print **large triangle** and 2 burgundy print **small triangles** together to make **Flying Geese**. Repeat with remaining triangles to make a total of 8 Flying Geese. Trim each Flying Geese to 5" x $2^3/_4$"; set aside.

Flying Geese (make 8)

making the hourglass blocks

1. Draw a diagonal line on wrong side of each remaining orange persimmon print, large floral print, and assorted orange, gold, pink, and red-orange **square**. With right sides together, place 1 marked square on top of 1 burgundy **square**. Stitch ¹/₄" from each side of drawn line (**Fig. 1**).
2. Cut along drawn line and press seam allowances toward the burgundy fabric to make 2 **Triangle-Squares**. Repeat to make 44 Triangle-Squares.
3. Referring to **Fig. 2**, draw a diagonal line on half of the Triangle-Squares. Referring to **Fig. 3**, match seams and place 1 marked and 1 unmarked Triangle-Square together, right sides together and with burgundy triangles opposite each other. Stitch ¹/₄" from each side of line. Cut apart on drawn line and press open to make 2 **Hourglass Blocks**. Make 44 Hourglass Blocks. Trim each Hourglass Block to 5" x 5"; set aside.

making the appliqué blocks

1. Fold and finger-press each burgundy **background square** vertically and horizontally to create placement guides. Arrange and fuse appliqués to 9 background squares. Arrange and fuse appliqués in reverse to remaining 9 background squares.
2. Follow **Satin Stitch Appliqué**, page 87, to stitch appliqués in place. Press from the wrong side of the background square. Trim each background square to 9¹/₂" x 9¹/₂".

Fig. 1

Triangle-Squares (make 44)

Fig. 2

Fig. 3

Hourglass Block (make 44)

assembling the quilt top

1. Sew 11 Hourglass Blocks and 2 Flying Geese together to make **Pieced Row**. Make 4 Pieced Rows.
2. Sew 6 Appliqué Blocks together to make **Appliquéd Row**. Make 3 Appliquéd Rows.
3. Sew Pieced Rows and Appliquéd Rows together to make quilt top center.
4. Refer to **Adding Mitered Borders**, page 89, to sew **inner borders** to quilt top center.
5. Refer to **Adding Squared Borders**, page 88, to sew **side** then **top** and **bottom outer borders** to quilt top. Press seam allowances towards outer border.

completing the quilt

1. Follow **Quilting**, page 90, to mark, layer, and quilt as desired. Quilt shown was machine quilted in the ditch around each appliqué in the Appliquéd Rows. A flower and leaf design is quilted vertically through the Pieced Row. A loop pattern is quilted in the inner border and an all-over swirl pattern is quilted in the outer border.
2. Use **binding square** and refer to **Making Continuous Bias Strip Binding**, page 93, to make 2¹/₄"w bias binding.
3. Follow **Attaching Binding With Mitered Corners**, page 94, to bind quilt.

Pieced Row
(make 4)

Appliqued Row
(make 3)

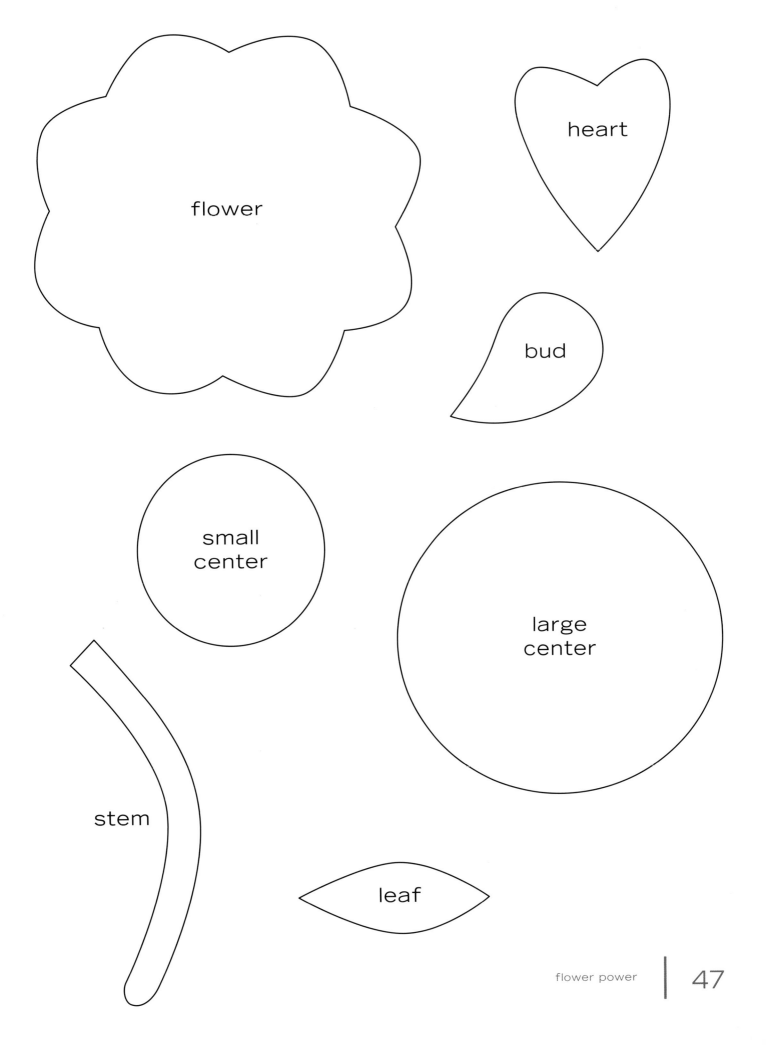

flower

heart

bud

small
center

large
center

stem

leaf

la costa
del sol

Finished Quilt Size: 87" x 87" (221 cm x 221 cm)
Finished Block Size: 10" x 10" (25 cm x 25 cm)

yardage requirements

Yardage is based on 43"/44" (109 cm/112 cm) wide fabric with a usable width of 40" (102 cm).

  $2^1/_8$ yds (1.9 m) of ivory print fabric for sashings and setting triangles B

  2 yds (1.8 m) of teal print fabric for sashings, inner borders, and binding

  $^1/_2$ yd (46 cm) of light print fabric for squares C and triangles D and E

  $2^1/_2$ yds (2.3 m) of green large print fabric for outer borders and squares A

  $^3/_8$ yd (34 cm) *each* of 8 assorted green, teal, and gold prints for squares A

  8 yds (7.3 m) of fabric for backing

You will also need:

  95" x 95" (241 cm x 241 cm) piece of batting

cutting the pieces

*Follow **Rotary Cutting**, page 84, to cut fabric. Cut all strips across the selvage-to-selvage width of the fabric. All measurements include $^1/_4$" seam allowances.*

From ivory print fabric:
- Cut 3 **narrow strips** $6^1/_2$"w.
- Cut 2 **wide strips** $8^1/_2$"w.
- Cut 4 squares $15^1/_2$" x $15^1/_2$". Cut each square in half **twice** diagonally to make 16 **setting triangles B**.

From teal print fabric:
- Cut 8 **strips** $2^1/_2$"w.
- Cut 4 **inner borders** $2^1/_4$" x 67", pieced as needed.
- Cut 2 strips $2^1/_4$"w. From these strips, cut 8 **rectangles G** $2^1/_4$" x $8^1/_2$".
- Cut 10 **binding strips** $2^1/_4$"w.

Continued on page 51.

cutting the pieces (cont.)

From light print fabric:
- Cut 2 strips 2¼"w. From these strips, cut 29 **squares C** 2¼" x 2¼".
- Cut 3 squares 3¾" x 3¾". Cut each square in half **twice** diagonally to make 12 **triangles D**.
- Cut 2 squares 2⅛" x 2⅛". Cut each square in half **once** diagonally to make 4 **triangles E**.

From green large print fabric:
- Cut 1 **strip** 10½"w. From this strip, cut 3 **squares A** 10½" x 10½".
- Cut 1 **strip** 8½"w. From this strip, cut 4 **squares F** 8½" x 8½".
- Cut 4 *lengthwise* **outer borders** 8½" x 67".

From *each* of 5 assorted green, teal, and gold prints:
- Cut 3 **squares A** 10½" x 10½".

From *each* of 3 assorted green, teal, and gold prints:
- Cut 2 **squares A** 10½" x 10½".

assembling the quilt top center

Follow **Machine Piecing** *and* **Pressing**, *page 85. Use a* ¼" *seam allowance.*

1. Sew 2 teal **strips** and 1 ivory **narrow strip** together to make **Strip Set A**. Press seam allowances toward teal fabric. Make 3 Strip Set A's. Cut across Strip Set A's at 2¼" intervals to make **Unit 1**. Make 36 Unit 1's.
2. Sew 1 teal **strip** and 1 ivory **wide strip** together to make **Strip Set B**. Press seam allowances toward teal fabric. Make 2 Strip Set B's. Cut across Strip Set B's at 2¼" intervals to make **Unit 2**. Make 28 Unit 2's.
3. Refer to **Assembly Diagram**, page 52, to lay out the **squares A**, **setting triangles B**, **Unit 1's**, **Unit 2's**, **squares C**, **triangles D**, and **triangles E**.
4. Assemble the Block Rows by alternately joining the **squares A** with the **Unit 1's** and **Unit 2's**. Press seam allowances toward the **squares A**. Complete the Block Rows by adding **setting triangles B** to the ends of each row.

5. Assemble the Sashing Rows by alternately joining the **Unit 1's** and **Unit 2's** with the **squares C**. Press seams toward the squares C. Complete the Sashing Rows by adding **triangles D** to the ends of each row.
6. Alternately sew the Block Rows and Sashing Rows together. Press the seam allowances toward the squares A. Sew **triangles E** to each corner of quilt top center.
7. Square quilt top center to 67" x 67".

adding the borders

1. Sew 1 teal **inner border** to the top and bottom of the quilt top center. Press seam allowances toward the inner border. Sew 1 **square C** to each end of the remaining teal inner borders. Press seam allowances toward the teal inner borders. Sew the inner borders to the sides of the quilt top center. Press seam allowances toward the teal inner border.

Strip Set A (make 3)   Unit 1 (make 36)

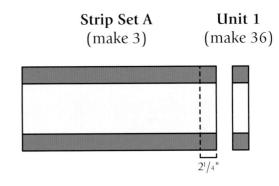

2¼"

Strip Set B (make 2)   Unit 2 (make 28)

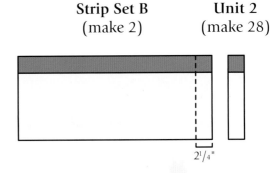

2¼"

2. Sew 1 **rectangle G** to each end of green large print **outer borders**. Press seam allowances toward the rectangles. Sew 1 outer border to each side of the quilt. Sew 1 **square F** to each end of the 2 remaining outer borders. Press seams toward the squares. Sew borders to the top and bottom of the quilt top.

finishing the quilt

1. Follow **Quilting**, page 90, to mark, layer, and quilt. Our quilt is machine quilted in the ditch along the sides of the inner border. The remainder of the quilt is quilted with an all-over swirl design.
2. Sew **binding strips** together end to end using diagonal seams (**Fig. 1**) to make a continuous binding strip.
3. Follow **Attaching Binding with Mitered Corners**, page 94, to bind quilt.

Assembly Diagram

Fig. 1

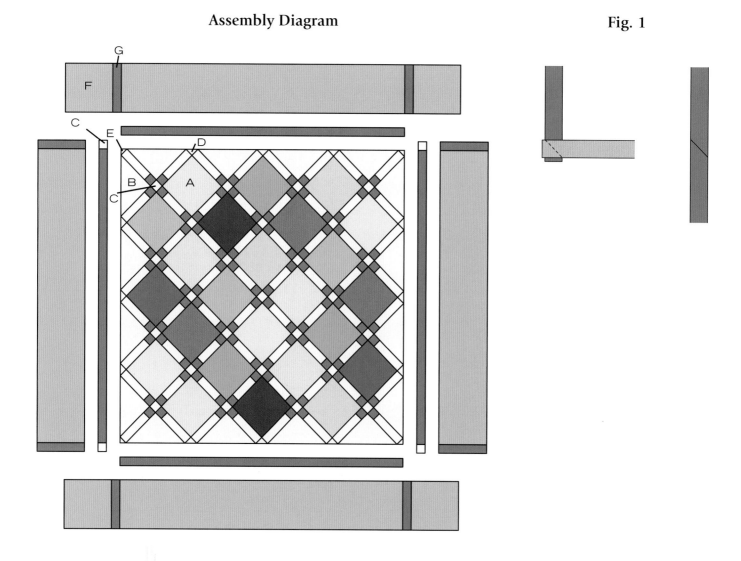

la costa del sol pillowcases

Approximate Size: 20" x 30" (51 cm x 76 cm)
shown on page 49

yardage requirements

Yardage is based on 43"/44" (109 cm/112 cm) wide fabric with a usable width of 40" (102 cm) and is adequate for making 2 pillowcases.

- 1⁵/₈ yds (1.5 m) of ivory print fabric
- ⁵/₈ yd (57 cm) of light green print fabric
- ¹/₄ yd (23 cm) of medium green print fabric

cutting the pieces

*Follow **Rotary Cutting**, page 84, to cut fabric. Fabrics are not always the same width from selvage to selvage. For the following pieces, determine the fabric that is the narrowest and trim remaining pieces to the same width. All measurements include ¹/₄" seam allowances.*

From ivory print fabric:
- Cut 2 **pillowcase bodies** 26¹/₂" x width of fabric.

From light green print fabric:
- Cut 2 **bands** 9³/₄" x width of fabric.

From medium green print fabric:
- Cut 2 **flanges** 2¹/₂" x width of fabric.

assembling the pillowcase

*Follow **Machine Piecing** and **Pressing**, page 85. Use a ¹/₄" seam allowance.*

1. Press 1 **flange** in half lengthwise. Press 1 long edge of 1 **band** ¹/₄" to wrong side.
2. With flange sandwiched in between and matching raw edges, pin right sides of band and **pillowcase body** together along 1 long edge.
3. Sew layers together along long edge. Press band away from pillowcase body. Press flange toward pillowcase body. Press seam allowances toward band.
4. Fold pillowcase in half. Aligning seams, sew along side and bottom.
5. Placing folded edge of band ¹/₂" beyond seamline, fold band to inside of pillowcase; pin. Turn pillowcase right side out. Catching folded edge of band in stitching, topstitch along flange ³/₈" from seamline.
6. Press pillowcase, pressing band flat.
7. Repeat Steps 1-6 for remaining pillowcase.

papillons

Finished Quilt Size: 42" x 42" (107 cm x 107 cm)
Finished Block Size: 12" x 12" (30 cm x 30 cm)

yardage requirements

Yardage is based on 42"/43" (109 cm/112 cm) wide fabric with a usable width of 40" (102 cm).

  1¹/₈ yds (1 m) of cream and turquoise butterfly print fabric for backgrounds

  1 yd (91 cm) of turquoise floral print fabric for appliqués and binding

  ³/₄ yd (69 cm) of green butterfly print fabric for appliqués and middle borders

  ³/₈ yd (34 cm) of brown butterfly print fabric for appliqués

  ³/₈ yd (34 cm) of brown floral print fabric for inner borders and appliqué

  ³/₄ yd (69 cm) of lime green floral print fabric for scallop appliqués and scalloped borders

  2⁷/₈ yds (2.6 m) of fabric for backing

You will also need:

  50" x 50" (127 cm x 127 cm) piece of batting

  Wrights EZ® Easy Scallop™ Adjustable Template by Darlene Zimmerman

  Paper-backed fusible web

  Twenty ⁵/₈" (16 mm) teal buttons

  Stabilizer

cutting the pieces

*Follow **Rotary Cutting**, page 84, to cut fabric. Cut all strips across the selvage-to-selvage width of the fabric. All measurements include ¹/₄" seam allowances.*

From cream and turquoise butterfly print fabric:

- Cut 2 strips 14"w. From these strips, cut 4 **large background squares** 14" x 14".
- Cut 2 strips 6"w. From these strips, cut 12 **small background squares** 6" x 6".

From turquoise floral print fabric:

- Cut 1 **binding square** 22" x 22".

From green butterfly print fabric:

- Cut 2 strips 4¹/₂"w. From these strips, cut 4 **middle borders** 4¹/₂" x 19¹/₂".

From brown floral print fabric:

- Cut 4 strips 2"w. From these strips, cut 2 **top/bottom inner borders** 2" x 24¹/₂" and 2 **side inner borders** 2" x 27¹/₂".

From lime green floral print fabric:

- Cut 4 strips 2"w. From these strips, cut 4 **rectangles** 2" x 25".
- Cut 4 strips 3¹/₂"w. From these strips, cut 2 **side outer borders** 3¹/₂" x 35¹/₂" and 2 **top/bottom outer borders** 3¹/₂" x 41¹/₂", pieced as needed.

cutting the appliqués

*Follow **Preparing Fusible Appliqués**, page 87, to use patterns, pages 62 - 63. **Note:** Appliqué patterns are printed in reverse.*

From turquoise floral print fabric:

- Cut 2 **A's**.
- Cut 2 **A's** in reverse.
- Cut 2 **B's**.
- Cut 2 **B's** in reverse.
- Cut 1 **F**.

From green butterfly print fabric:

- Cut 2 **A's**.
- Cut 2 **A's** in reverse.
- Cut 2 **B's**.
- Cut 2 **B's** in reverse.

From brown butterfly print fabric:

- Cut 4 **C's**.
- Cut 4 **C's** in reverse.
- Cut 4 **D's**.
- Cut 12 **H's**.
- Cut 12 **H's** in reverse.

From brown floral print fabric:

- Cut 1 **E**.

From lime green floral print fabric:

- Cut 1 **G**.
- Cut 4 strips of fusible web 2" x 27¹/₂". For each scallop appliqué, trace wall hanging scallop pattern, page 63, for a total of 5 scallops, onto fusible web. Fuse web to wrong side of **rectangle**. Cut 4 **scallop appliqués**.

making the blocks and borders

1. For **Butterfly Block**, fold and finger-press each **large background square** diagonally to create a placement guide. Arrange and fuse 1 set of appliqués **A – D** to each large background square.

2. For **Corner Block**, fold and finger-press each **small background square** diagonally to create placement guide. Arrange and fuse appliqués **H** and **H in reverse** to each small background square.

3. For **Scalloped Borders**, fold and finger-press each **inner border** in the center to create a placement guide. Center and fuse 1 **scallop appliqué** to one long edge of each inner border.

4. Follow **Satin Stitch Appliqué**, page 87, to stitch appliqués in place. Press from the wrong side of the blocks and borders. Trim each large Butterfly Block to $12^1/_2$" x $12^1/_2$". Trim each Corner Block to $4^1/_2$" x $4^1/_2$".

Butterfly Block

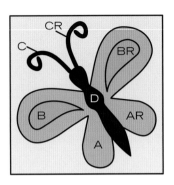

Corner Block

Scalloped Borders

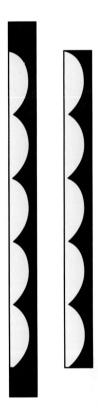

assembling the quilt top center

Follow **Machine Piecing** *and* **Pressing**, *page 85, to assemble the quilt top. Refer to* **Quilt Top Diagram** *for placement.*

1. For Quilt Top Center, sew **Butterfly Blocks** together.
2. Center and fuse appliqués **E – G** over seamlines in center of Quilt Top Center.
3. Satin stitch appliqués in place.

adding the borders

1. Matching centers and corners, sew **top/bottom scalloped borders** to Quilt Top Center. Press seam allowances toward quilt top center.
2. Matching centers and corners, sew **side scalloped borders** to Quilt Top Center. Press seam allowances toward quilt top center.
3. Noting orientation of blocks, sew 1 Corner Block to each end of 2 **middle borders**. Press seam allowances toward borders. Sew 1 middle border to each side of quilt top, pressing seam allowances toward quilt top center.
4. Noting orientation of blocks, sew 2 Corner Blocks to *each* end of the 2 remaining middle borders. Press seam allowances toward outermost Corner Blocks. Sew middle borders to top and bottom of quilt top, pressing seams toward quilt top center.
5. Sew **side outer borders** to quilt top. Press seam allowances toward outer borders.
6. Sew **top/bottom outer borders** to quilt top center. Press seam allowances toward outer borders.

completing the quilt

1. Follow manufacturer's instructions and use scallop tool to mark 5 full scallops along each side of quilt top. Stitch along the marked scallop line. **Do not** trim at this point.
2. Follow **Quilting**, page 90, to mark, layer, and quilt as desired. **Do not** quilt beyond the marked scalloped edge. Quilt shown is machine quilted in the ditch along each border. There is wavy channel quilting in the middle border and a feather pattern in the outer border. The remainder of the quilt is quilted with a meandering swirl pattern.
3. Use **binding square** and follow **Making Continuous Bias Strip Binding**, page 93, to make 2¼"w bias binding.
4. Matching **wrong** sides, press binding in half. Press one end of binding diagonally. Beginning with pressed end, align raw edges of binding with the marked scallop line and begin stitching with a ¹/₄" seam allowance at the top of a scallop. Stitch to the base of the "V," stop with the needle down at that point. Lift presser foot, pivot the quilt and binding, and then stitch out of the "V," taking care not to stitch in any pleats. Continue around the quilt, easing the binding around the curves until binding overlaps beginning end by approximately 2". Trim excess binding.
5. Trim the quilt even with the raw edges of the binding. Fold binding to the back and use a Blindstitch to stitch in place, allowing the inside corners to fold over on themselves.
6. Sew a button in the center of each scallop on the inner border, being careful not to stitch all the way through to the back of the quilt.

Quilt Top Diagram

Quilt Assembly Diagram

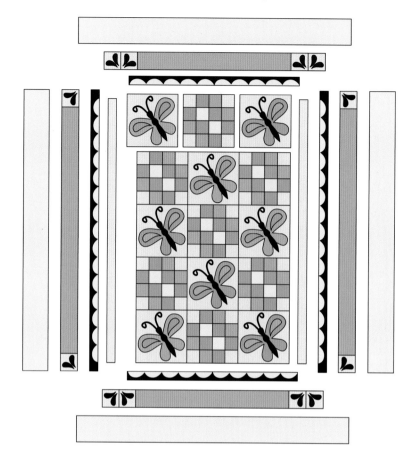

Alternate Size

Finished Size	Twin Size: 65" x 85" (165 cm x 216 cm)
Blocks	Block Size: 12" x 12" (30 cm x 30 cm) Block Layout: 15 (3 x 5)
Fabric	2^1/$_2$ yds (2.3 m) of cream and turquoise butterfly print fabric for backgrounds, 16-Patch Blocks, and spacers 1^3/$_4$ yds (1.6 m) of turquoise floral print fabric for 16-Patch Blocks, appliqués, and binding 1^1/$_2$ yds (1.4 m) of green butterfly print fabric for 16-Patch Blocks, middle borders, and appliqués ^{1}/$_4$ yd (23 cm) of brown butterfly print fabric for appliqués ^{1}/$_2$ yd (46 cm) of brown floral print fabric for inner borders 2^3/$_8$ yds (2.2 m) of lime green floral print fabric for 16-Patch Blocks, scallop appliqués, and outer borders 5^1/$_4$ yds (4.8 m) of fabric for backing
You will also need	73" x 93" (185 cm x 236 cm) piece of batting Wrights EZ® Easy Scallop™ Adjustable Template by Darlene Zimmerman Paper-backed fusible web Stabilizer

Cut pieces	**From cream and turquoise butterfly print fabric:** Cut 3 strips 14"w. From these strips, cut 8 **large background squares** 14" x 14". Cut 2 strips 6"w. From these strips, cut 12 **small background squares** 6" x 6". Cut 4 **strips** $3^1/2$"w for 16-Patch blocks.* Cut 2 **spacers** $2^1/2$" x $60^1/2$", pieced as needed. **From turquoise floral print fabric:** Cut 6 **strips** $3^1/2$"w for 16-Patch blocks.* Cut **binding square** 30" x 30" for $2^1/4$"w continuous bias binding. **From green butterfly print fabric:** Cut 4 **strips** $3^1/2$"w for 16-Patch blocks.* Cut 2 **top/bottom middle borders** $4^1/2$" x $36^1/2$". Cut 2 **side middle borders** $4^1/2$" x $56^1/2$", pieced as needed. **From brown floral print fabric:** Cut 2 top/bottom **inner borders** $2^1/2$" x $40^1/2$" and 2 **side inner borders** $2^1/2$" x $64^1/2$", pieced as needed. **From lime green floral print fabric:** Cut 2 **strips** $3^1/2$"w for 16-Patch blocks.* Cut 2 **rectangles** $2^1/2$" x $40^1/2$" and 2 **rectangles** $2^1/2$" x $60^1/2$", pieced as needed. Cut 2 **side outer borders** $6^1/2$" x $72^1/2$" and 2 **top/bottom outer borders** $6^1/2$" x $64^1/2$", pieced as needed. *Use strips to make 2 strip sets of each color placement with 4 strips each. Note color placement on Quilt Assembly Diagram. Cut strip sets at $3^1/2$" intervals to make 14 pieced strips of each color combination. Join 4 pieced strips to make 16-Patch block. Make 7 16-Patch blocks.
Cut appliqués	**From *each* of turquoise floral print and green butterfly print fabrics:** Cut 4 A's. Cut 4 A's in reverse. Cut 4 B's. Cut 4 B's in reverse. **From brown butterfly print fabric:** Cut 8 C's. Cut 8 C's in reverse. Cut 8 D's. Cut 12 H's. Cut 12 H's in reverse. **From lime green floral print fabric:** Cut 2 strips of fusible web $2^1/2$" x $40^1/2$" and 2 strips of fusible web $2^1/2$" x $60^1/2$". For each top/bottom scallop appliqué, trace twin size scallop pattern, page 63, for a total of 10 scallops onto fusible web. Fuse web to wrong side of shorter rectangles. Cut 2 top/bottom scallop appliqués. For each side scallop appliqué, trace scallop pattern for a total of 15 scallops onto fusible web. Cut 2 side scallop appliqués.

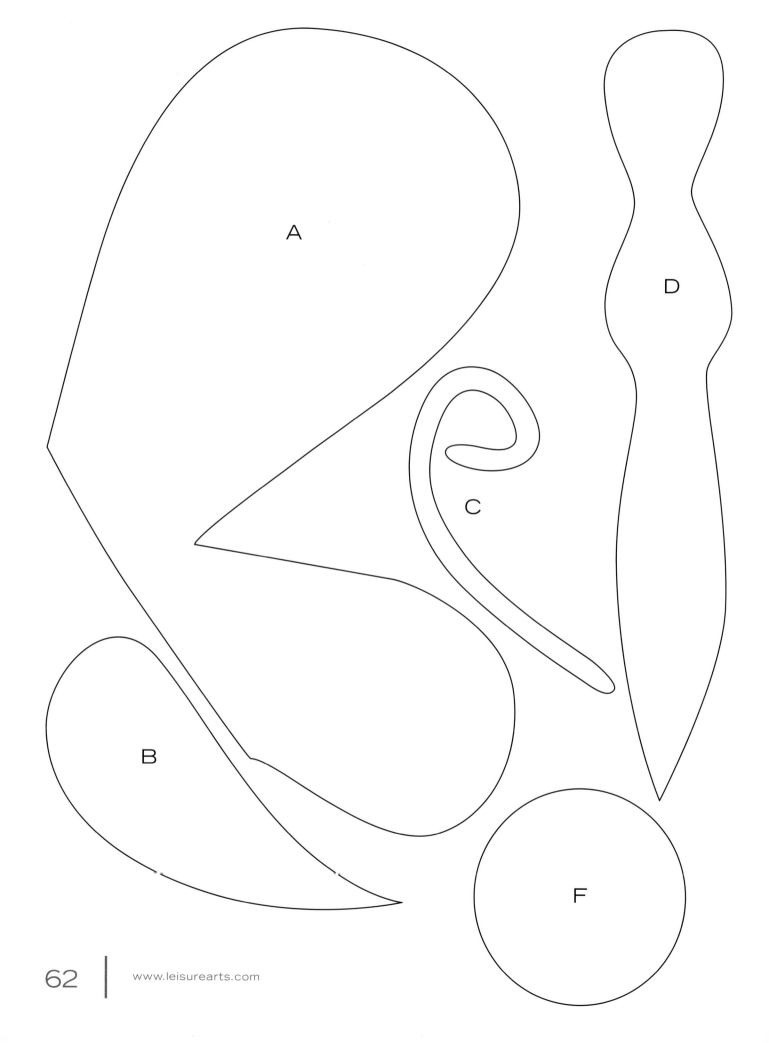

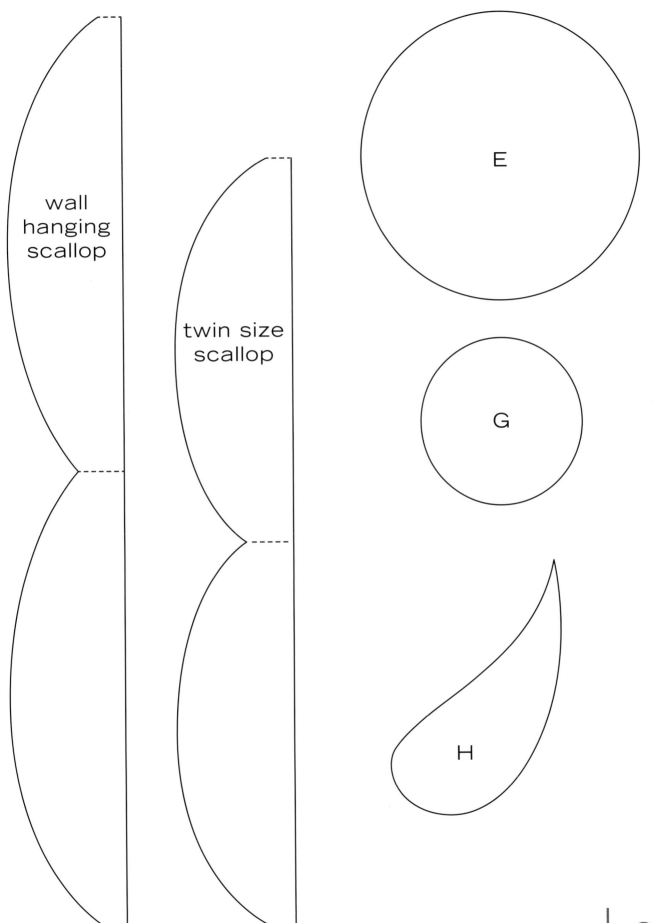

wall
hanging
scallop

twin size
scallop

E

G

H

playa
del sol

Finished Quilt Size: 74" x 92" (188 cm x 234 cm)
Finished Block Size: 9" x 9" (23 cm x 23 cm)

yardage requirements

Yardage is based on 43"/44" (109 cm/112 cm) wide fabric with a usable width of 40" (102 cm).

- $^5/_8$ yd (57 cm) **each** of 10 assorted blue print fabrics
- $3^1/_8$ yds (2.9 m) of light blue print fabric for background
- $1^1/_4$ yds (1.1 m) of blue stripe fabric for borders
- $6^7/_8$ yds (6.3 m) of fabric for backing
- $^5/_8$ yd (57 cm) of fabric for binding

You will also need:
- 82" x 100" (208 cm x 254 cm) piece of batting

cutting the pieces

*Follow **Rotary Cutting**, page 84, to cut fabric. Cut all strips across the selvage-to-selvage width of the fabric. Borders include extra length for "insurance" and will be trimmed after assembling quilt top center. All measurements include $^1/_4$" seam allowances.*

From *each* of 10 assorted blue print fabrics:
- Cut 2 strips 3"w. From these strips, cut 15 **squares A** 3" x 3".
- Cut 1 strip 8"w. From this strip, cut 10 **rectangles B** 3" x 8".
- Cut 1 strip $1^1/_2$"w. From this strip, cut 3 **rectangles E** $1^1/_2$" x $9^1/_2$". You will use 28 and have 2 left over.

From remaining fabrics:
- Cut a *total* of 4 assorted **rectangles G** $1^1/_2$" x $2^1/_2$".
- Cut a *total* of 4 assorted **squares H** $1^1/_2$" x $1^1/_2$".
- Cut a *total* of 4 assorted **rectangles J** $1^1/_2$" x $4^1/_2$".

Continued on page 67.

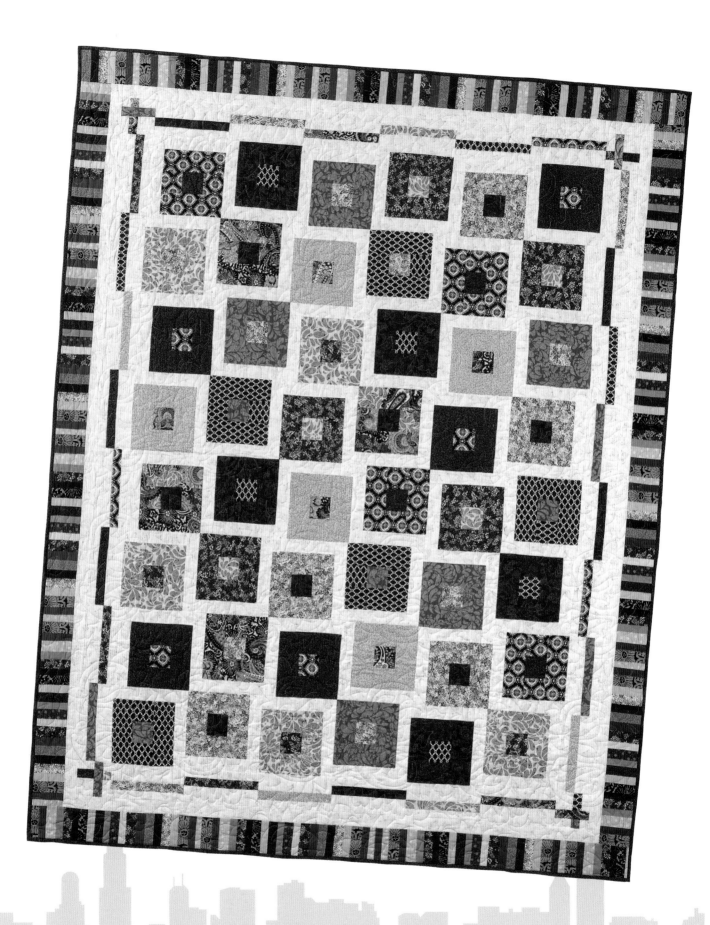

cutting the pieces (cont.)

From light blue print fabric for background:
- Cut 2 **side inner borders** 2" x 84^1/$_2$", pieced as needed.
- Cut 2 **top/bottom inner borders** 2" x 69^1/$_2$", pieced as needed.
- Cut 3 strips 8"w. From these strips, cut 48 **rectangles C** 2" x 8".
- Cut 6 strips 9^1/$_2$"w. From these strips, cut 48 **rectangles D** 2" x 9^1/$_2$", 28 **rectangles E** 1^1/$_2$" x 9^1/$_2$" and 28 **rectangles F** 2^1/$_2$" x 9^1/$_2$".
- Cut 8 **rectangles G** 1^1/$_2$" x 2^1/$_2$".
- Cut 4 **squares H** 1^1/$_2$" x 1^1/$_2$".
- Cut 4 **squares I** 2^1/$_2$" x 2^1/$_2$".

From blue stripe fabric for borders:
- Cut 2 **side outer borders** 4^1/$_2$" x 87^1/$_2$", pieced as needed.
- Cut 2 **top/bottom outer borders** 4^1/$_2$" x 77^1/$_2$", pieced as needed.

From fabric for binding:
- Cut 9 **binding strips** 2^1/$_4$"w.

making the center blocks

*Follow **Machine Piecing** and **Pressing**, page 85, to assemble the quilt top. Each block consists of 2 squares A and 2 rectangles B from 1 fabric, 1 contrasting square A, and white print rectangles C and D. The cutting instructions provide you with a few extra A and B pieces so that you can mix and match in order to get the look you want.*

1. Sew 2 matching **squares A** and 1 contrasting **square A** together to make **Unit 1**. Press seam allowances away from the center square A.
2. Sew 1 **rectangle B** to opposite sides of Unit 1 to make **Unit 2**. Press seam allowances toward rectangle B's.
3. Sew 1 **rectangle C** to one side of Unit 2, pressing seam allowances toward rectangle C. Sew 1 **rectangle D** to adjacent side of Unit 2 to make **Center Block**. Press seam allowances toward rectangle D. Make 48 Center Blocks.

making the border blocks

1. Sew 1 white and 1 blue **rectangle E** and 1 **rectangle F** together to make **Border Block**. Press all seam allowances toward rectangle F. Make 28 Border Blocks.

Unit 1 (make 48)

Unit 2 (make 48)

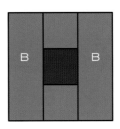

Center Block (make 48)

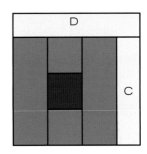

Border Block (make 28)

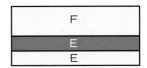

making the corner blocks

1. Sew 2 contrasting **squares H** and 1 **rectangle G** together to make **Unit 3**. Make 4 Unit 3's.
2. Sew 2 contrasting **rectangles G** and 1 **square I** together to make **Unit 4**. Make 4 Unit 4's.
3. Sew 1 **Unit 3**, 1 **Unit 4**, and 1 rectangle **J** together to make **Corner Block**. Make 4 Corner Blocks.

assembling the quilt top center

*Refer to **Quilt Top Assembly Diagram** to assemble the quilt top.*

1. Rotating blocks as shown, lay out the Center Blocks in 8 Rows of 6 Blocks each.
2. Rotating Blocks as shown, lay out the Border Blocks.
3. Sew Border Blocks and Corner Blocks together to make top and bottom Rows. Sew Center Blocks and Border Blocks together to make remaining Rows. Sew Rows together to make quilt top center.

adding the borders

1. Refer to **Adding Squared Borders**, page 88, to sew **side**, then **top** and **bottom inner borders** to quilt top center. Press seam allowances toward borders.
2. Sew **side**, then **top** and **bottom outer borders** to quilt top in same manner as inner borders. Press seam allowances toward outer borders.

completing the quilt

1. Follow **Quilting**, page 90, to mark, layer, and quilt as desired. Quilt shown was machine quilted with an all-over floral design.
2. Sew **binding strips** together end to end using a diagonal seam (**Fig. 1**) to make a continuous binding strip.
3. Follow **Attaching Binding With Mitered Corners**, page 94, to bind quilt.

Unit 3 (make 4)

Unit 4 (make 4)

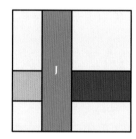

Corner Block (make 4)

Fig. 1

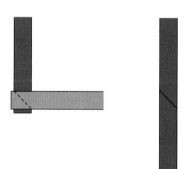

Quilt Top Assembly Diagram

	Throw Size: 56" x 74" (142 cm x 188 cm)	King Size: 92" x 92" (234 cm x 234 cm)
Finished Size	Throw Size: 56" x 74" (142 cm x 188 cm)	King Size: 92" x 92" (234 cm x 234 cm)
Blocks	Block Size: 9" x 9" (23 cm x 23 cm) Block Layout: 24 (4 x 6)	Block Size: 9" x 9" (23 cm x 23 cm) Block Layout: 64 (8 x 8)
Fabric	10 assorted blue print fat quarters 2$\frac{1}{8}$ yds (1.9 m) of light blue print fabric 1 yd (91 cm) of blue stripe fabric 4$\frac{5}{8}$ yds (4.2 m) of fabric for backing $\frac{5}{8}$ yd (57 cm) of fabric for binding	$\frac{1}{2}$ yd (46 cm) *each* of 12 assorted blue print fabrics 3$\frac{3}{4}$ yds (3.4 m) of light blue print fabric 1$\frac{3}{8}$ yds (1.3 m) of blue stripe fabric 8$\frac{3}{8}$ yds (7.7 m) of fabric for backing $\frac{3}{4}$ yd (69 cm) of fabric for binding
You will also need	64" x 82" (163 cm x 208 cm) piece of batting	100" x 100" (254 cm x 254 cm) piece of batting
Cut pieces	**From assorted blue print fat quarters:** Cut 24 matching sets of 2 **squares A** 3" x 3" and 2 **rectangles B** 3" x 8". Cut 24 contrasting **squares A** 3" x 3". Cut 20 **rectangles E** 1$\frac{1}{2}$" x 9$\frac{1}{2}$". Cut 4 **rectangles G** 1$\frac{1}{2}$" x 2$\frac{1}{2}$". Cut 4 **squares H** 1$\frac{1}{2}$" x 1$\frac{1}{2}$". Cut 4 **rectangles J** 1$\frac{1}{2}$" x 4$\frac{1}{2}$".	**From assorted blue print fabrics:** Cut 64 matching sets of 2 **squares A** 3" x 3" and 2 **rectangles B** 3" x 8". Cut 64 contrasting **squares A** 3" x 3". Cut 32 **rectangles E** 1$\frac{1}{2}$" x 9$\frac{1}{2}$". Cut 4 **rectangles G** 1$\frac{1}{2}$" x 2$\frac{1}{2}$". Cut 4 **squares H** 1$\frac{1}{2}$" x 1$\frac{1}{2}$". Cut 4 **rectangles J** 1$\frac{1}{2}$" x 4$\frac{1}{2}$".

Cut pieces (cont.)		
	From light blue print fabric: Cut 2 **side inner borders** 2" x $66^1/_2$", pieced as needed.	**From light blue print fabric:** Cut 2 **side inner borders** 2" x $84^1/_2$", pieced as needed.
	Cut 2 **top/bottom inner borders** 2" x $51^1/_2$", pieced as needed.	Cut 2 **top/bottom inner borders** 2" x $87^1/_2$", pieced as needed.
	Cut 2 strips 8"w. From these strips, cut 24 **rectangles C** 2" x 8".	Cut 4 strips 8"w. From these strips, cut 64 **rectangles C** 2" x 8".
	Cut 4 strips $9^1/_2$"w. From these strips, cut 24 **rectangles D** 2" x $9^1/_2$", 20 **rectangles E** $1^1/_2$" x $9^1/_2$", and 20 **rectangles F** $2^1/_2$" x $9^1/_2$".	Cut 7 strips $9^1/_2$"w. From these strips, cut and 64 **rectangles D** 2" x $9^1/_2$", 32 **rectangles E** $1^1/_2$" x $9^1/_2$", and 32 **rectangles F** $2^1/_2$" x $9^1/_2$".
	Cut 8 **rectangles G** $1^1/_2$" x $2^1/_2$".	Cut 8 **rectangles G** $1^1/_2$" x $2^1/_2$".
	Cut 4 **squares H** $1^1/_2$" x $1^1/_2$".	Cut 4 **squares H** $1^1/_2$" x $1^1/_2$".
	Cut 4 **squares I** $2^1/_2$" x $2^1/_2$".	Cut 4 **squares I** $2^1/_2$" x $2^1/_2$".
	From blue stripe fabric: Cut 2 **side outer borders** $4^1/_2$" x $69^1/_2$", pieced as needed.	**From blue stripe fabric:** Cut 2 **side outer borders** $4^1/_2$" x $87^1/_2$", pieced as needed.
	Cut 2 **top/bottom outer borders** $4^1/_2$" x $59^1/_2$", pieced as needed.	Cut 2 **top/bottom outer borders** $4^1/_2$" x $95^1/_2$", pieced as needed.
	From fabric for binding: Cut 8 **binding strips** $2^1/_4$"w.	**From fabric for binding:** Cut 10 **binding strips** $2^1/_4$"w.

tenderness

Finished Wallhanging Size: 27" x 27" (69 cm x 69 cm)
Finished Block Size: 4" x 4" (10 cm x 10 cm)

yardage requirements

Yardage is based on 42"/43" (109 cm/112 cm) wide fabric with a usable width of 40" (102 cm).

- $^1/_4$ yd (23 cm) **each** of 4 assorted red print fabrics
- 8" x 8" (20 cm x 20 cm) square of pink print fabric
- 12" x 12" (30 cm x 30 cm) square of green print fabric
- 6" x 6" (15 cm x 15 cm) square of stripe fabric
- 1 yd (91 cm) (80 cm) of black print fabric
- 1 yd (91 cm) of fabric for backing

You will also need:

- 35" x 35" (89 cm x 89 cm) piece of batting
- Paper-backed fusible web
- Stabilizer

cutting the pieces

*Follow **Rotary Cutting**, page 84, to cut fabric. Cut all strips across the selvage-to-selvage width of the fabric. All measurements include $^1/_4$" seam allowances.*

From red print #1 fabric:

- Cut 3 **strips #1** $1^1/_2$"w.

From red print #2 fabric:

- Cut 3 **strips #2** $1^1/_2$"w.

From red print #3 fabric:

- Cut 3 **strips #3** $1^1/_2$"w.

From red print #4 fabric:

- Cut 3 **strips #4** $1^1/_2$"w.

From black print fabric:

- Cut 1 **background square** $17^1/_2$" x $17^1/_2$".
- Cut 2 **side outer borders** $1^1/_2$" x $24^1/_2$".
- Cut 2 **top/bottom outer borders** $1^1/_2$" x $26^1/_2$".
- Cut 3 **binding strips** $2^1/_4$"w.

cutting the appliqués

*Follow **Preparing Fusible Appliqués**, page 87, to use patterns, pages 76 - 77. **Note:** Appliqué patterns are printed in reverse.*

From red print #1 fabric:
- Cut 1 heart **A**.

From red print #2 fabric:
- Cut 2 hearts **B**.

From red print #3 fabric:
- Cut 2 hearts **C**.

From pink print fabric:
- Cut 2 hearts **A**.

From green print fabric:
- Cut 1 leaf **D** and 1 leaf **D in reverse**.
- Cut 1 leaf **E** and 1 leaf **E in reverse**.
- Cut 3 stems **F** $^1/_2$" x 9".

From stripe fabric:
- Cut 1 vase **G**.

making the center block

Refer to **Quilt Top Diagram**, page 76.

1. Fold and finger-press **background square** vertically to create placement guide. Arrange and fuse appliqués **A** – **G** to background square.
2. Follow **Satin Stitch Appliqué**, page 87, to stitch appliqués in place. Press from the wrong side of the background square. Trim background square to $16^1/_2$" x $16^1/_2$".

making the rail fence blocks

*Follow **Machine Piecing** and **Pressing**, page 85, to assemble the quilt top. Use a $^1/_4$" seam allowance.*

1. Sew 1 *each* of **strips #1 - #4** together in numerical order to make **Strip Set**. Press all seam allowances in 1 direction. Make 3 Strip Sets. Cut across Strip Set at $4^1/_2$" intervals to make 20 Unit 1's.

assembling the quilt top

1. Rotating Units, sew 4 **Unit 1's** together to make **side border**. Make 2 side borders.
2. Sew 1 side border to opposite sides of background square.
3. Rotating Units, sew 6 **Unit 1's** together to make **top border**. Repeat to make **bottom border**.
4. Sew top and bottom borders to background square to make quilt top center.
5. Sew **side** then **top** and **bottom outer borders** to quilt top center.

completing the quilt

1. Follow **Quilting**, page 90, to mark, layer, and quilt as desired. Quilt shown was machine quilted with outline quilting around the appliqués and meandering quilting in the borders.
2. Sew **binding strips** together end to end using a diagonal seam (**Fig. 1**) to make a continuous binding strip.
3. Follow **Attaching Binding With Mitered Corners**, page 94, to bind quilt.

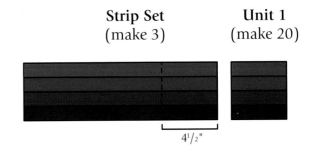

Strip Set (make 3)   Unit 1 (make 20)

$4^1/_2$"

Fig. 1

Quilt Top Diagram

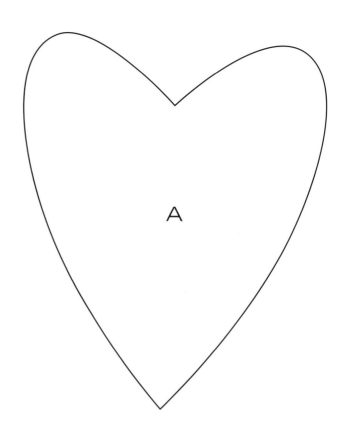

A

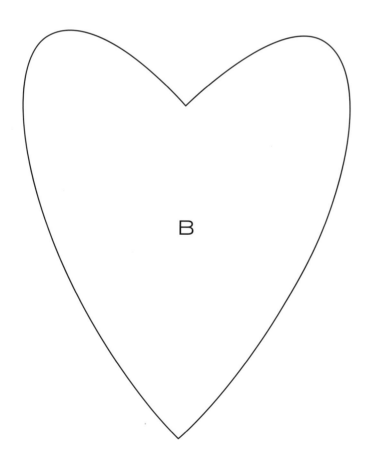

B

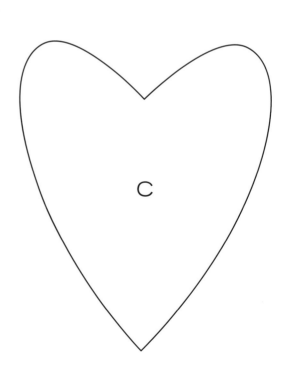

C

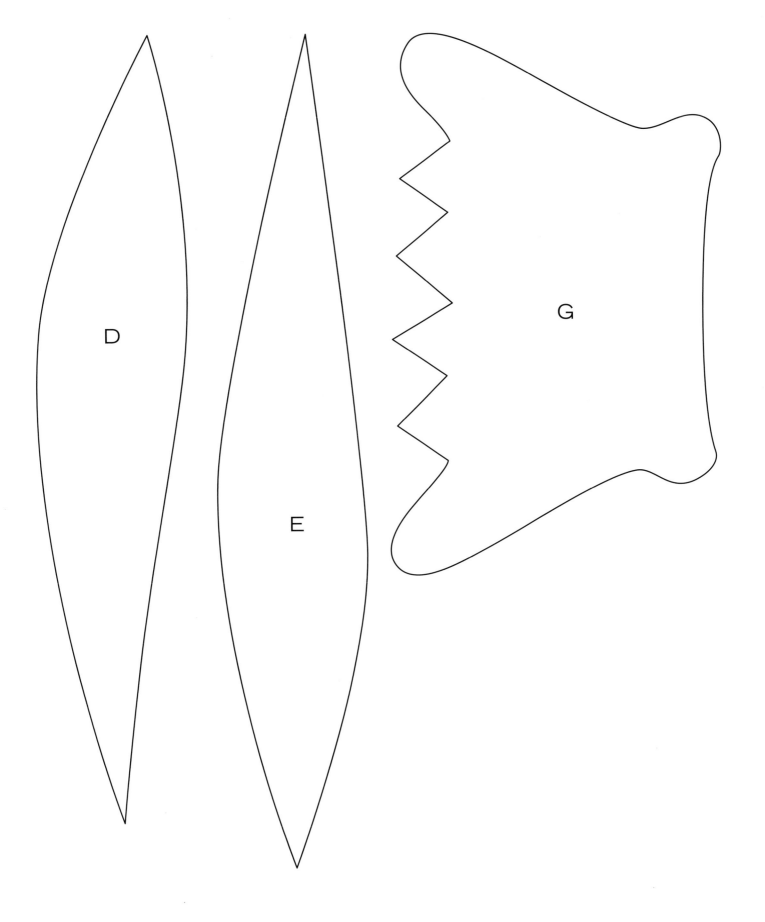

D

E

G

city leaves

Finished Wallhanging Size: 31" x 43" (79 cm x 109 cm)
Finished Block Size: 6" x 9" (15 cm x 23 cm)

yardage requirements

Yardage is based on 42"/43" (109 cm/112 cm) wide fabric with a usable width of 40" (102 cm). A fat quarter measures approximately 21" x 18" (53 cm x 46 cm).

10 assorted coordinating fat quarters
$1/2$ yd (46 cm) of black tone-on-tone print fabric
$1^1/2$ yds (1.4 m) of fabric for backing
$3/8$ yd (34 cm) of fabric for binding

You will also need:
39" x 51" (99 cm x 130 cm) piece of batting
Paper-backed fusible web
Stabilizer

cutting the pieces

*Follow **Rotary Cutting**, page 84, to cut fabric. Cut all strips across the selvage-to-selvage width of the fabric. All measurements include $1/4$" seam allowances.*

From assorted coordinating fat quarters:
- Cut 16 **backgrounds** 7" x 10".

From black tone-on-tone print fabric:
- Cut 2 **side borders** $3^1/2$" x $36^1/2$".
- Cut 2 **top/bottom borders** $3^1/2$" x $30^1/2$".

From fabric for binding:
- Cut 5 **binding strips** $2^1/4$"w.

cutting the appliqués

*Follow **Preparing Fusible Appliqués**, page 87, to use patterns, page 82. **Note:** Appliqué patterns are printed in reverse.*

From assorted coordinating fat quarters:
- Cut 16 **leaves**.
- Cut 16 **stems**.

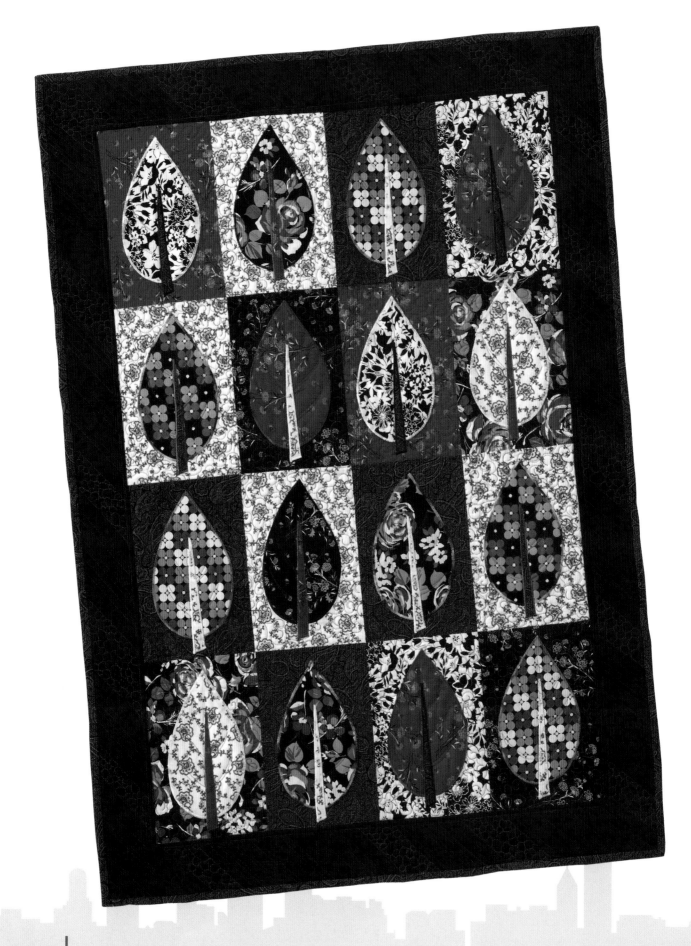

making the leaf blocks

1. Fold and finger-press each **background** vertically and horizontally to create placement guides. Arrange and fuse **leaf** and **stem** appliqués on **background**.
2. Follow **Satin Stitch Appliqué**, page 87, to stitch appliqués in place. Press from the wrong side of the background. Trim backgrounds to 6¹/₂" x 9¹/₂" to make **Leaf Blocks**.

assembling the quilt top

*Follow **Machine Piecing** and **Pressing**, page 85, to assemble the quilt top. Refer to **Quilt Top Diagram** for placement.*
1. Sew 4 Leaf Blocks together to make a Row. Make 4 Rows. Sew Rows together to make quilt top center.
2. Sew 1 **side border** to each side of quilt top center. Sew **top** and **bottom borders** to quilt top center.

completing the quilt

1. Follow **Quilting**, page 90, to mark, layer, and quilt as desired. Quilt shown is machine quilted in the ditch along each border and along each stem. There is also outline quilting along each border. Free-form veins are quilted on each leaf and the background of each block is quilted with a meandering swirl pattern. There are random diagonal lines and diagonal areas of bubbles quilted in each border.
2. Sew **binding strips** together end to end using a diagonal seam (**Fig. 1**) to make a continuous binding strip.
3. Follow **Attaching Binding With Mitered Corners**, page 94, to bind quilt.

Quilt Top Diagram

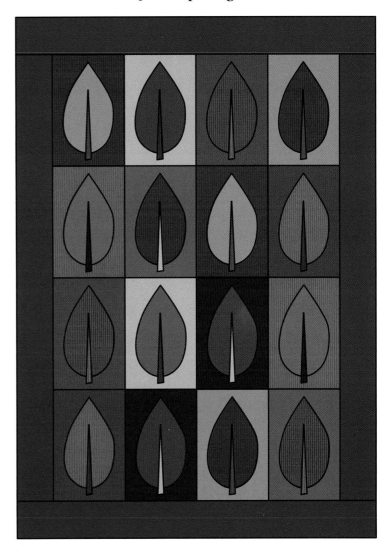

Fig. 1

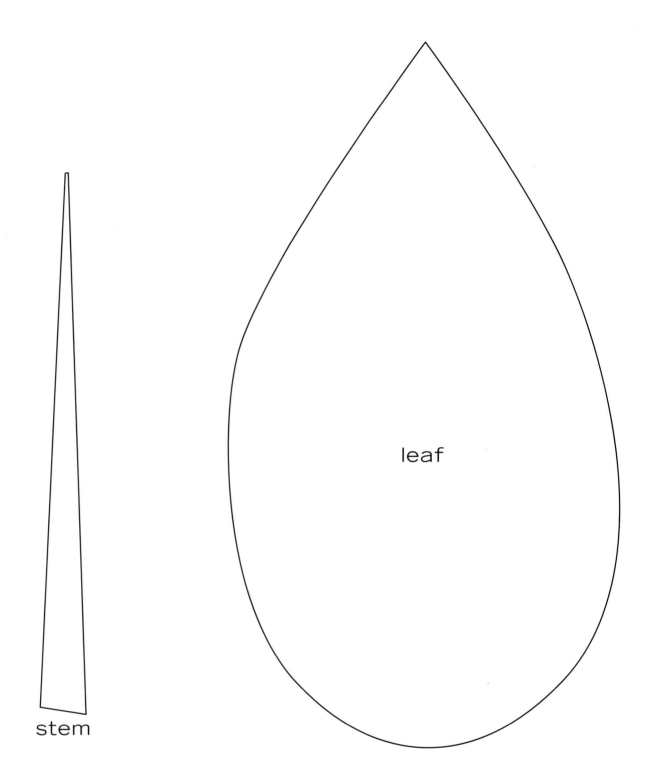

stem

leaf

general instructions

To make your quilting easier and more enjoyable, we encourage you to carefully read all of the general instructions, study the color photographs, and familiarize yourself with the individual project instructions before beginning a project.

fabrics

selecting fabrics

Choose high-quality, medium-weight 100% cotton fabrics. All-cotton fabrics hold a crease better, fray less, and are easier to quilt than cotton/polyester blends.

Yardage requirements listed for each project are based on 43"/44" wide fabric with a "usable" width of 40" after shrinkage and trimming selvages. Actual usable width will probably vary slightly from fabric to fabric. Our recommended yardage lengths should be adequate for occasional re-squaring of fabric when many cuts are required.

preparing fabrics

Pre-washing fabrics may cause edges to ravel. As a result, your pre-cut fabric pieces may not be large enough to cut all of the pieces required for your chosen project. Therefore, we do not recommend pre-washing your yardage or pre-cut fabrics.

Before cutting, prepare fabrics with a steam iron set on cotton and starch or sizing. The starch or sizing will give the fabric a crisp finish. This will make cutting more accurate and may make piecing easier.

rotary cutting

cutting from yardage

- Place fabric on work surface with fold closest to you.

- Cut all strips from the selvage-to-selvage width of the fabric.

- Square left edge of fabric using rotary cutter and rulers (**Figs. 1 - 2**).

- To cut each strip required for a project, place ruler over cut edge of fabric, aligning desired marking on ruler with cut edge; make cut (**Fig. 3**).

- When cutting several strips from a single piece of fabric, it is important to make sure that cuts remain at a perfect right angle to the fold; square fabric as needed.

cutting from fat quarters

- Place fabric flat on work surface with lengthwise (short) edge closest to you.

- Cut all strips parallel to the long edge of fabric in the same manner as cutting from yardage.

- To cut each strip required for a project, place ruler over cut edge of fabric, aligning desired marking on ruler with cut edge; make cut.

Fig. 1

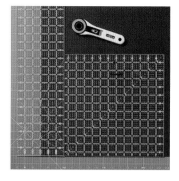

Fig. 2

Fig. 3

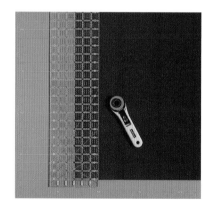

machine piecing

Precise cutting, followed by accurate piecing, will ensure that all pieces of quilt top fit together well.

- Set sewing machine stitch length for approximately 11 stitches per inch.

- Use neutral-colored general-purpose sewing thread (not quilting thread) in needle and in bobbin.

- An accurate $1/4$" seam allowance is *essential*. Presser feet that are $1/4$" wide are available for most sewing machines.

- When piecing, always place pieces right sides together and match raw edges; pin if necessary.

- Chain piecing saves time and will usually result in more accurate piecing.

- Trim away points of seam allowances that extend beyond edges of sewn pieces.

sewing strip sets

When there are several strips to assemble into a strip set, first sew strips together into pairs, then sew pairs together to form strip set. To help avoid distortion, sew seams in opposite directions (**Fig. 4**).

sewing across seam intersections

When sewing across intersection of two seams, place pieces right sides together and match seams exactly, making sure seam allowances are pressed in opposite directions (**Fig. 5**).

sewing sharp points

To ensure sharp points when joining triangular or diagonal pieces, stitch across the center of the "X" (shown in pink) formed on wrong side by previous seams (**Fig. 6**).

pressing

- Use steam iron set on "Cotton" for all pressing.

- Press after sewing each seam.

- Seam allowances are almost always pressed to one side, usually toward the darker fabric. However, to reduce bulk it may occasionally be necessary to press seam allowances toward the lighter fabric or even to press them open.

- To prevent a dark fabric seam allowance from showing through light fabric, trim darker seam allowance slightly narrower than lighter seam allowance.

- To press long seams, such as those in long strip sets, without curving or other distortion, lay strips across width of the ironing board.

Fig. 4

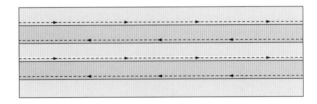

Fig. 5

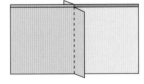

Fig. 6

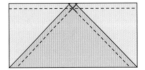

appliqué

needle-turn appliqué

Making and Using Templates

Patterns for Needle-Turn Appliqué do not include seam allowances.

1. To make a template from a pattern, use a permanent fine-point pen to carefully trace pattern onto template plastic, making sure to transfer any markings. Cut out template along outer drawn line. Check template against original pattern for accuracy.

2. Place template on right side of appliqué fabric. Lightly draw around template with pencil, leaving at least 1" between shapes. Repeat for number of shapes specified in project instructions. Cut out shapes approximately $^3/_{16}$" outside drawn line.

Needle-Turn Appliqué

Using your needle to turn under the seam allowance while blindstitching (page 96) an appliqué piece to the background fabric is called "needle-turn" appliqué.

1. Thread a sharps needle with a single strand of general-purpose sewing thread that matches appliqué; knot one end.

2. Begin blindstitching on as straight an edge as possible, turning a small section of $^3/_{16}$" seam allowance to wrong side with needle, concealing drawn line (**Fig. 7**). Clip curves as needed, up to but not through drawn line.

3. To stitch outward points, stitch to $^1/_2$" from point (**Fig. 8**). Turn seam allowance under at point (**Fig. 9**); then turn remainder of seam allowance between stitching and point. Stitch to point, taking two or three stitches at top of point to secure. Turn under small amount of seam allowance past point and resume stitching.

4. To stitch inward point, stitch to $^1/_2$" from point (**Fig. 10**). Clip to but not through seam allowance at point (**Fig. 11**). Turn seam allowance under between stitching and point. Stitch to point, taking two or three stitches at point to secure. Turn under small amount of seam allowance past point and resume stitching.

5. Do not turn under or stitch seam allowances that will be covered by other appliqué pieces.

6. For appliqué pieces that are layered (such as a flower center on top of a flower), appliqué top piece to bottom piece before appliquéing bottom piece to background.

7. To appliqué pressed bias strips, baste strips in place and blindstitch along edges.

8. To reduce bulk, background fabric behind appliqués may be cut away. After stitching appliqués in place, turn background over and use sharp scissors or specially designed appliqué scissors to trim away background fabric approximately $^1/_4$" from stitching line. Take care not to cut appliqué fabric or stitches. Bulk may be reduced behind layered appliqués by cutting away bottom layer of appliqués.

Fig. 7

Fig. 8   Fig. 9

Fig. 10   Fig. 11

machine appliqué

Preparing Fusible Appliqués

White or light-colored fabrics may need to be lined with fusible interfacing before applying fusible web to prevent darker fabrics from showing through.

1. Place paper-backed fusible web, paper side up, over appliqué pattern. Trace pattern onto paper side of web with pencil as many times as indicated in project instructions for a single fabric.
2. Follow manufacturer's instructions to fuse traced patterns to wrong side of fabrics. Do not remove paper backing. (*Note:* Some pieces may be given as measurements, such as a 2" x 4" rectangle, instead of drawn patterns. Fuse web to wrong side of fabrics indicated for these pieces.)
3. Use scissors to cut out appliqué pieces along traced lines; use rotary cutting equipment to cut out appliqué pieces given as measurements. Remove paper backing from all pieces.

Satin Stitch Appliqué

A good satin stitch is a thick, smooth, almost solid line of zigzag stitching that covers the exposed raw edges of appliqué pieces.

1. Pin stabilizer, such as paper or any of the commercially available products, on wrong side of background fabric before stitching appliqués in place.
2. Thread sewing machine with general-purpose thread; use general-purpose thread that matches background fabric in bobbin.
3. Set sewing machine for a medium (approximately $1/8$") zigzag stitch and a short stitch length. Slightly loosening the top tension may yield a smoother stitch.
4. Begin by stitching two or three stitches in place (drop feed dogs or set stitch length at 0) to anchor thread. Most of the Satin Stitch should be on the appliqué with the right edge of the stitch falling at the outside edge of the appliqué. Stitch over all exposed raw edges of appliqué pieces.

5. (*Note:* Dots on **Figs. 12 – 17** indicate where to leave needle in fabric when pivoting.) For outside corners, stitch just past corner, stopping with needle in background fabric (**Fig. 12**). Raise presser foot. Pivot project, lower presser foot, and stitch adjacent side (**Fig. 13**).
6. For inside corners, stitch just past corner, stopping with needle in appliqué fabric (**Fig. 14**). Raise presser foot. Pivot project, lower presser foot, and stitch adjacent side (**Fig. 15**).
7. When stitching outside curves, stop with needle in background fabric. Raise presser foot and pivot project as needed. Lower presser foot and continue stitching, pivoting as often as necessary to follow curve (**Fig. 16**).

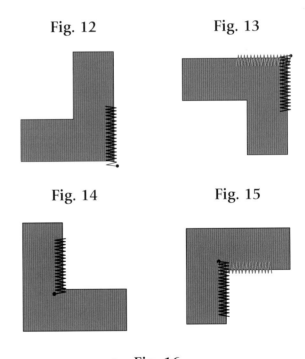

Fig. 12   **Fig. 13**

Fig. 14   **Fig. 15**

Fig. 16

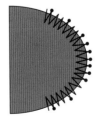

8. When stitching inside curves, stop with needle in appliqué fabric. Raise presser foot and pivot project as needed. Lower presser foot and continue stitching, pivoting as often as necessary to follow curve (**Fig. 17**).
9. Do not backstitch at end of stitching. Pull threads to wrong side of background fabric; knot thread and trim ends.
10. Carefully tear away stabilizer.

borders

adding squared borders

In most cases, our instructions for cutting borders include an extra 2" of length at each end for "insurance;" borders will be trimmed after measuring completed center section of quilt top.

1. Mark the center of each edge of quilt top.
2. Squared borders are usually added to sides, then top and bottom edges of the quilt top center. To add side borders, lay quilt top center on a flat surface; measure across quilt top center to determine length of borders (**Fig. 18**). Trim side borders to the determined length.
3. Mark center of 1 long edge of side border. Matching center marks and raw edges, pin border to quilt top, easing in any fullness; stitch. Press seam allowances toward the border.
4. Measure across center of quilt top, including attached borders, to determine length of top and bottom borders (**Fig. 19**). Trim top/bottom borders to the determined length. Repeat Step 3 to add borders to quilt top.

Fig. 17

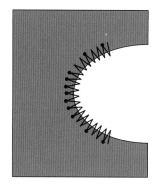

Fig. 18

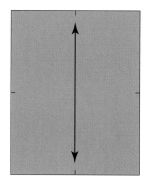

Fig. 19

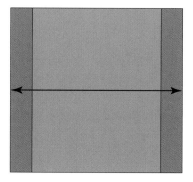

adding mitered borders

1. Mark the center of each edge of quilt top (see **Fig. 18**).

2. Mark center of 1 long edge of top border. Measure across center of quilt top. Matching center marks and raw edges, pin border to center of quilt top edge. From center of border, measure out $^1/_2$ the width of the quilt top in both directions and mark. Match marks on border with corners of quilt top and pin. Easing in any fullness, pin border to quilt top between center and corners. Sew border to quilt top, beginning and ending seams exactly $^1/_4$" from each corner of quilt top and backstitching at beginning and end of stitching (**Fig. 20**).

3. Repeat Step 2 to sew bottom, then side borders, to center section of quilt top. To temporarily move first 2 borders out of the way, fold and pin ends as shown in **Fig. 21**.

4. Fold 1 corner of quilt top diagonally with right sides together; use rotary cutting ruler to mark stitching line as shown in **Fig. 22**. Pin strips together along drawn line. Sew on drawn line, backstitching at beginning and end of stitching (**Fig. 23**).

5. Turn mitered corner right side up. Check to see that there is not a gap at the inner end of the seam and that corner does not pucker.

6. Trim seam allowances to $^1/_4$"; press to 1 side.

7. Repeat Steps 4-6 to miter each remaining corner.

Fig. 20

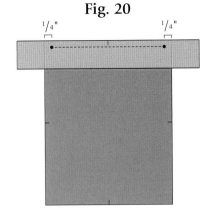

Fig. 21

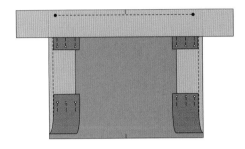

Fig. 22

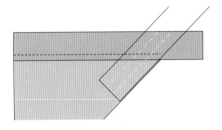

Fig. 23

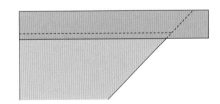

quilting

*Quilting holds the three layers (top, batting, and backing) of the quilt together and can be done by hand or machine. Because marking, layering, and quilting are interrelated and may be done in different orders depending on circumstances, please read entire **Quilting** section, pages 90 – 92, before beginning project.*

types of quilting designs

In the Ditch Quilting
Quilting along seamlines or along edges of appliquéd pieces is called "in the ditch" quilting. This type of quilting should be done on side **opposite** seam allowance and does not have to be marked.

Outline Quilting
Quilting a consistent distance, usually $1/4$", from seam or appliqué is called "outline" quilting. Outline quilting may be marked, or $1/4$" masking tape may be placed along seamlines for quilting guide. (Do not leave tape on quilt longer than necessary, since it may leave an adhesive residue.)

Motif Quilting
Quilting a design, such as a feathered wreath, is called "motif" quilting. This type of quilting should be marked before basting quilt layers together.

Echo Quilting
Quilting that follows the outline of an appliquéd or pieced design with two or more parallel lines is called "echo" quilting. This type of quilting does not need to be marked.

Channel Quilting
Quilting with straight, parallel lines is called "channel" quilting. This type of quilting may be marked or stitched using a guide.

Crosshatch Quilting
Quilting straight lines in a grid pattern is called "crosshatch" quilting. Lines may be stitched parallel to edges of quilt or stitched diagonally. This type of quilting may be marked or stitched using a guide.

Meandering Quilting
Quilting in random curved lines and swirls is called "meandering" quilting. Quilting lines should not cross or touch each other. This type of quilting does not need to be marked.

Stipple Quilting
Meandering quilting that is very closely spaced is called "stipple" quilting. Stippling will flatten the area quilted and is often stitched in background areas to raise appliquéd or pieced designs. This type of quilting does not need to be marked.

marking quilting lines
Quilting lines may be marked using fabric marking pencils, chalk markers, water- or air-soluble pens.

Simple quilting designs may be marked with chalk or chalk pencil after basting. A small area may be marked, then quilted, before moving to next area to be marked. Intricate designs should be marked before basting using a more durable marker.

Caution: Pressing may permanently set some marks. Test different markers **on scrap fabric** to find one that marks clearly and can be thoroughly removed.

A wide variety of pre-cut quilting stencils, as well as entire books of quilting patterns, are available. Using a stencil makes it easier to mark intricate or repetitive designs.

To make a stencil from a pattern, center template plastic over pattern and use a permanent marker to trace pattern onto plastic. Use a craft knife with single or double blade to cut channels along traced lines (**Fig. 24**).

Fig. 24

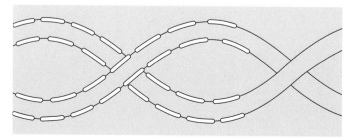

preparing the backing

To allow for slight shifting of quilt top during quilting, backing should be approximately 4" larger on all sides. Yardage requirements listed for quilt backings are calculated for 43"/44"w fabric. Using 90"w or 108"w fabric for the backing of a bed-sized quilt may eliminate piecing. To piece a backing using 43"/44"w fabric, use the following instructions.

1. Measure length and width of quilt top; add 8" to each measurement.
2. If determined width is 79" or less, cut backing fabric into two lengths slightly longer than determined *length* measurement. Trim selvages. Place lengths with right sides facing and sew long edges together, forming tube (**Fig. 25**). Match seams and press along one fold (**Fig. 26**). Cut along pressed fold to form single piece (**Fig. 27**).
3. If determined width is more than 79", it may require less fabric yardage if the backing is pieced horizontally. Divide determined *length* measurement by 40" to determine how many widths will be needed. Cut required number of widths the determined *width* measurement. Trim selvages. Sew long edges together to form single piece.
4. Trim backing to size determined in Step 1; press seam allowances open.

Fig. 25	Fig. 26	Fig. 27

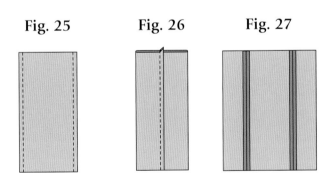

choosing the batting

The appropriate batting will make quilting easier. All cotton or cotton/polyester blend battings work well for machine quilting because the cotton helps "grip" quilt layers.

Types of batting include cotton, polyester, wool, cotton/polyester blend, cotton/wool blend, and silk.

When selecting batting, refer to package labels for characteristics and care instructions. Cut batting same size as prepared backing.

assembling the quilt

1. Examine wrong side of quilt top closely; trim any seam allowances and clip any threads that may show through to the front of the quilt. Press quilt top, being careful not to "set" any marked quilting lines.
2. Place backing *wrong* side up on flat surface. Use masking tape to tape edges of backing to surface. Place batting on top of backing fabric. Smooth batting gently, being careful not to stretch or tear. Center quilt top *right* side up on batting.
3. Use 1" rustproof safety pins to "pin-baste" all layers together, spacing pins approximately 4" apart. Begin at center and work toward outer edges to secure all layers. If possible, place pins away from areas that will be quilted, although pins may be removed as needed when quilting.

machine quilting methods

Use general-purpose thread in bobbin. **Do not** use quilting thread. Thread the needle of machine with general-purpose thread or transparent monofilament thread to make quilting blend with quilt top fabrics. Use decorative thread, such as a metallic or contrasting-color general-purpose thread, to make quilting lines stand out more.

Straight-Line Quilting

The term "straight-line" is somewhat deceptive, since curves (especially gentle ones) as well as straight lines can be stitched with this technique.

1. Set stitch length for six to ten stitches per inch and attach walking foot to sewing machine.

2. Determine which section of quilt will have longest continuous quilting line, oftentimes area from center top to center bottom. Roll up and secure each edge of quilt to help reduce the bulk, keeping fabrics smooth. Smaller projects may not need to be rolled.

3. Begin stitching on longest quilting line, using very short stitches for the first $1/4$" to "lock" quilting. Stitch across project, using one hand on each side of walking foot to slightly spread fabric and to guide fabric through machine. Lock stitches at end of quilting line.

4. Continue machine quilting, stitching longer quilting lines first to stabilize quilt before moving on to other areas.

Free-Motion Quilting

Free-motion quilting may be free form or may follow a marked pattern.

1. Attach darning foot to sewing machine and lower or cover feed dogs.

2. Position quilt under darning foot; lower foot. Holding top thread, take a stitch and pull bobbin thread to top of quilt. To "lock" beginning of quilting line, hold top and bobbin threads while making three to five stitches in place.

3. Use one hand on each side of darning foot to slightly spread fabric and to move fabric through the machine. Even stitch length is achieved by using smooth, flowing hand motion and steady machine speed. Slow machine speed and fast hand movement will create long stitches. Fast machine speed and slow hand movement will create short stitches. Move quilt sideways, back and forth, in a circular motion, or in a random motion to create desired designs; do not rotate quilt. Lock stitches at end of each quilting line.

making a hanging sleeve

Attaching a hanging sleeve to the back of a wall hanging or quilt before the binding is added allows the project to be displayed on a wall.

1. Measure width of quilt top edge and subtract 1". Cut piece of fabric 7"w by determined measurement.

2. Press short edges of fabric piece $1/4$" to wrong side; press edges $1/4$" to wrong side again and machine stitch in place.

3. Matching wrong sides, fold piece in half lengthwise to form a tube.

4. Follow project instructions to sew binding to quilt top and to trim backing and batting. Before Blindstitching binding to backing, match raw edges and stitch hanging sleeve to center top edge on back of quilt.

5. Finish binding quilt, treating hanging sleeve as part of backing.

6. Blindstitch bottom of hanging sleeve to backing, taking care not to stitch through to front of quilt.

7. Insert a dowel or slat into hanging sleeve.

binding

Binding encloses the raw edges of the quilt. Because of its stretchiness, bias binding works well for binding projects with curves or rounded corners and tends to lie smooth and flat in any given circumstance. Binding may also be cut from straight lengthwise or crosswise grain of fabric.

making continuous bias strip binding

Bias strips for binding can simply be cut and pieced to desired length. However, when a long length of binding is needed, the "continuous" method is quick and accurate.

1. Use square cut from binding fabric called for in project instructions. Cut square in half diagonally to make two triangles.
2. With right sides together and using a $1/4$" seam allowance, sew triangles together (**Fig. 28**); press seam allowances open.
3. On wrong side of fabric, draw lines the width of the binding as specified in project instructions, usually $2^1/4$"(**Fig. 29**). Cut off any remaining fabric less than this width.
4. With right sides inside, bring short edges together to form a tube; match raw edges so that first drawn line of top section meets second drawn line of bottom section (**Fig. 30**).
5. Carefully pin edges together by inserting pins through drawn lines at point where drawn lines intersect, making sure pins go through intersections on both sides. Using a $1/4$" seam allowance, sew edges together; press seam allowances open.
6. To cut continuous strip, begin cutting along first drawn line (**Fig. 31**). Continue cutting along drawn line around tube.
7. Trim ends of bias strip square.

Fig. 28

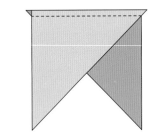

Fig. 29

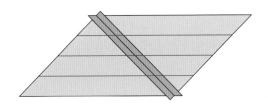

Fig. 30

Fig. 31

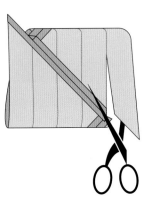

attaching binding with mitered corners

1. Matching wrong sides and raw edges, press strip in half lengthwise to complete binding.

2. Beginning with one end near center on bottom edge of quilt, lay binding around quilt to make sure that seams in binding will not end up at a corner. Adjust placement if necessary. Matching raw edges of binding to raw edge of quilt top, pin binding to right side of quilt along one edge.

3. When you reach first corner, mark $^1/_4$" from corner of quilt top (**Fig. 32**).

4. Beginning approximately 10" from end of binding and using a $^1/_4$" seam allowance, sew binding to quilt, backstitching at beginning of stitching and at mark (**Fig. 33**). Lift needle out of fabric and clip thread.

5. Fold binding as shown in **Figs. 34 – 35** and pin binding to adjacent side, matching raw edges. When you've reached the next corner, mark $^1/_4$" from edge of quilt top.

6. Backstitching at edge of quilt top, sew pinned binding to quilt (**Fig. 36**); backstitch at the next mark. Lift needle out of fabric and clip thread.

7. Continue sewing binding to quilt, stopping approximately 10" from starting point (**Fig. 37**).

Fig. 32

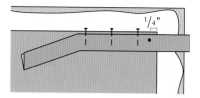

Fig. 33

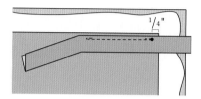

Fig. 34　　　**Fig. 35**

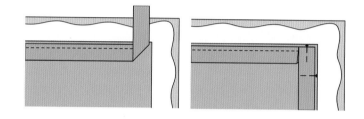

Fig. 36

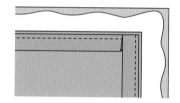

Fig. 37

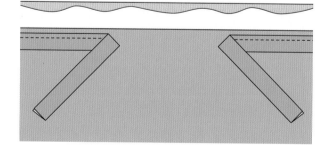

8. Bring beginning and end of binding to center of opening and fold each end back, leaving a $^1/_4$" space between folds (**Fig. 38**). Finger press folds.

9. Unfold ends of binding and draw a line across wrong side in finger-pressed crease. Draw a line through the lengthwise pressed fold of binding at the same spot to create a cross mark. With edge of ruler at cross mark, line up 45° angle marking on ruler with one long side of binding. Draw a diagonal line from edge to edge. Repeat on remaining end, making sure that the two diagonal lines are angled the same way (**Fig. 39**).

10. Matching right sides and diagonal lines, pin binding ends together at right angles (**Fig. 40**).

11. Machine stitch along diagonal line (**Fig. 41**), removing pins as you stitch.

12. Lay binding against quilt to double check that it is correct length.

13. Trim binding ends, leaving $^1/_4$" seam allowance; press seam open. Stitch binding to quilt.

14. If using $2^1/_2$"w binding (finished size $^1/_2$"), trim backing and batting a scant $^1/_4$" larger than quilt top so that batting and backing will fill the binding when it is folded over to quilt backing. If using narrower binding, trim backing and batting even with edges of quilt top.

Fig. 38

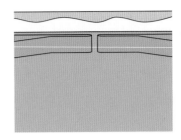

Fig. 39

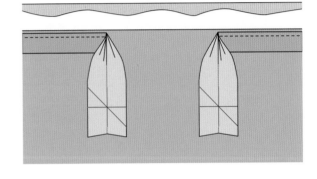

Fig. 40

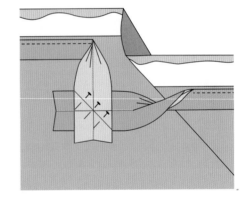

Fig. 41

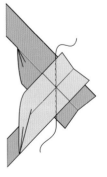

15. On one edge of quilt, fold binding over to quilt backing and pin pressed edge in place, covering stitching line (**Fig. 42**). On adjacent side, fold binding over, forming a mitered corner (**Fig. 43**). Repeat to pin remainder of binding in place.
16. Blindstitch binding to backing, taking care not to stitch through to front of quilt.

blind stitch

Come up at 1, go down at 2, and come up at 3 (**Fig. 44**). Length of stitches may be varied as desired.

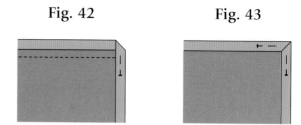

Fig. 42   **Fig. 43**

Fig. 44

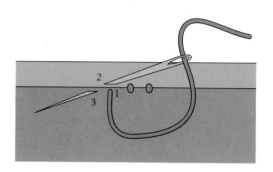

Metric Conversion Chart	
Inches x 2.54 = centimeters (cm)	Yards x .9144 = meters (m)
Inches x 25.4 = millimeters (mm)	Yards x 91.44 = centimeters (cm)
Inches x .0254 = meters (m)	Centimeters x .3937 = inches (")
	Meters x 1.0936 = yards (yd)

Standard Equivalents					
¹⁄₈"	3.2 mm	0.32 cm	¹⁄₈ yard	11.43 cm	0.11 m
¹⁄₄"	6.35 mm	0.635 cm	¹⁄₄ yard	22.86 cm	0.23 m
³⁄₈"	9.5 mm	0.95 cm	³⁄₈ yard	34.29 cm	0.34 m
¹⁄₂"	12.7 mm	1.27 cm	¹⁄₂ yard	45.72 cm	0.46 m
⁵⁄₈"	15.9 mm	1.59 cm	⁵⁄₈ yard	57.15 cm	0.57 m
³⁄₄"	19.1 mm	1.91 cm	³⁄₄ yard	68.58 cm	0.69 m
⁷⁄₈"	22.2 mm	2.22 cm	⁷⁄₈ yard	80 cm	0.8 m
1"	25.4 mm	2.54 cm	1 yard	91.44 cm	0.91 m